AF450262

I-Chingmancy

Yoruba Lucumi 16 Oracle Geomancy with I Ching Enhancement

Sixto J. Novaton
(BabaSixto IfaOdara)

Blue Ocean Press
Japan & USA

Copyright @ 2023 Blue Ocean Press
All Rights Reserved.

This publication may not be reproduced, stored in a retrieval system or transmitted in any form or by any means, electronic, mechanical, photocopying, recording, or otherwise, without prior written permission of the publisher, except by a reviewer who may quote brief passages in a review to be printed in a periodical.

Published by:
Blue Ocean Press

Japan Office
6F & 7F TOC Daiichi Bldg.
1-8-3 Shibuya
Shibuya-ku, Tokyo, Japan 150-0002

USA Office
P.O. Box 510818
Punta Gorda, FL 33951 USA

URL: http://www.blueoceanpublications.com
Email: director@aoishima-research.org

ISBN: 978-4-902837-30-8

Table of Contents

Introduction

This book integrates the Ifa 16 Major Oracles of 256 Ifa Signs (16 x 16 System) with the 64 I-Ching Hexagrams (8 x 8 System) to allow readers to function with both systems independently.

The Ifa Intellectual System was inscribed in 2008 on UNESCO's Representative List of the Intangible Cultural Heritage of the Humanity (originally proclaimed in 2005). UNESCO describes the Ifa divination system as follows: "The Ifa divination system, which makes use of an extensive corpus of texts and mathematical formulas, is practiced among Yoruba communities and by the African diaspora in the Americas and the Caribbean. The word Ifa refers to the mystical figure Ifa or Orunmila, regarded by the Yoruba as the deity of wisdom and intellectual development.

In contrast to other forms of divination in the region that employ spirit mediumship, Ifa divination does not rely on a person having oracular powers but rather on a system of signs that are interpreted by a diviner, the Ifa priest or babalawo, literally "the priest's father". The Ifa divination system is applied whenever an important individual or collective decision has to be made.

The Ifa literary corpus, called odu, consists of 256 parts subdivided into verses called ese, whose exact number is unknown as they are constantly increasing (there are around 800 ese per odu). Each of the 256 odu has its specific divination signature, which is determined by the babalawo using sacred palm-nuts and a divination chain. The ese, considered the most important part of Ifa divination, are chanted by the priests in poetic language. The ese reflect Yoruba history, language, beliefs, cosmovision and contemporary social issues. The knowledge of Ifa has been preserved within Yoruba communities and transmitted among Ifa priests."

According to Yoruba tradition, Orunmila was the being present at the time of Creation (Big Bang), therefore having knowledge of the blueprint of the universe. The Big Bang is described as the Odu, the Original Mother, the Mother of All Creation, as the Cosmic Womb that give birth to the forces of expansion and contraction that comprise the universe. These forces, which can be understood as binary in nature, assembled into 16 metaphysical patterns. From these 16 emerged another 240 combinations of expansion and contraction. These principles range from pure light (pure expansion) to pure darkness (pure contraction). We are the living embodiments of these metaphysical principles.

Through research, it has been found that Ifa was developed over 11,000 years ago in Northeast Africa, known today as Ethiopia, and referred to historically in various sources as Axum, Aker, Somaliland, Kush or Punt. Over time, the wisdom of Ifa spread across Africa, and to Asia. The original eight-bit form of Ifa is still practiced today in Nigeria among the Yoruba and Benin Edo who call it 'Ifa'; in Benin/Dahomey among the Fon who call it 'Fa'; in Togo and Ghana among the Ewe who call it 'Afa'; in North Africa among the Arabs who call it 'Ilm al Raml' (Science of the Sand) or 'Khatt al Raml' (Lines in the Sand); in Madagascar among the Malagasy who call is Sikidy; and among the people of the African Diaspora located through North America, South America, and the Caribbean, found in the traditions of Santeria, Candomble, Macumba, and Vodou.

It is noted in the Yoruba tradition that Orunmila visited China and shared this system with the Chinese people. It is postulated that I-ching, a six-bit binary system, is a subset of Ifa that arrived in China between 5,300 and 6,000 years ago.

Ifa, Taoism, and Veda are considered Sister Intellectual Systems, all describing the universe and its function through similar mathematical systems.

8

Part 1
Divination System

How to Read the Coconut Toss - Obtaining an oracle for divination

This simple system is a summarized extract of accumulated knowledge from when I first began to toss obi (coconuts) at 16. Granted, it has been expanded with in signs from the cowrie (dilogun) and IFa systems of divination. It has been written for those whom after having dedicated much time to spiritual enlightenment, now have a need to verify their communication through a simple 'yes' or 'no' questioning system. Plainly, there are those who do not have an affinity with any divination system. So, I have put together this system of 16 basic signs that will support the communication necessary for any individual to obtain answers, the rest is up to the individuals' merited grace and intuition. This system will also expand an individual's medium development through devotion and practice.

To be utilized are four circular coconut shells, 4 coins , or 4 cowrie shells. As long as the objects are of the same type, shape, and one side can be identified as facing upward (1), and the bottom side (0). The written format are indicative of the toss being read from bottom to top, and right to left. For the sake of maintaining this system simple (i.e. not limiting to nay specific set of divinities) all divinities which an individual has forged a relationship through their merits, will speak to them through this system. All that is needed is an invocation prayer that they have an affinity with, in order to call upon them, and establish a linked communication.

Advice: never take interpretations ultra-literally: there are moment where it will hit head one; other moments to be expanded and your unique condition supplying the detail. Attempt to apply each sign what is relevant to what you are living or asking at the moment. This system forms a base towards the learning of the more complex Yoruba Lucumi system of divination, especially for those wishing to continue into priest(ess) hood in the Yoruba Lucumi Santeria religion. It will not replace the proficiency of divination performed by a fully qualified Yoruba Orisha, or Ifa priest in time of needed specialized ritual work for difficult resolutions to problems.

Consecration of Religious Objects for Divination

Find a religious pagan, or Santeria priest/tess practitioner, who can consecrate your divination objects: 4 coins, 4 coconut shells, or 4 cowrie shells.

Place the consecrated objects on your shrine and proceed to spiritual devotion through weekly prayer and meditation ritual. An individual needs to out in the time in attaining spiritual grace, enlightenment, and merit the divine forces attention. This is not overnight task. It can take months and years of devotion in order to merit to correct communication. Always look to receive mentorship from an experienced priest-ess. It is imperative that you do, so as to not open a can of worms, and then not know how to resolve situations.

The time will come for you to experiment. I am of the belief in obtaining experience and getting to know your spiritual connection to divinities and forces on your own, but through much guidance and discipline. There is no one better than yourself who knows of the life struggles, which leads to an understanding of whom your spirit guides are. Yet, without mentorship many more mistakes can be made leading to slower development, so never stop trying to find the right person to connect with. When working to achieve meeting the right mentor, pray and meditate to your ancestors and spirit guides to lead you to the correct person.

Way of Using the System

Have a special mat that will be used exclusively for tossing your objects on to. Place a glass of water next to it. Then proceed to reciting your invocation prayer as accustomed and according to the belief system in which you are obtaining training or being mentored. Included here is a Yoruba mojuba, as well as a spiritual prayer, which I used many years ago when I used to cast the I-Ching coins. Then proceed to tossing the objects:

Ways of Tossing

First Way

Ask a question then toss the objects to obtain a simple "Yes" or "NO" by just reading the sign as 1 of 5 answers; the answers being Alafia, Eyeife, Itawa, Okana Sodde, or Okana Yekun. Only take the advice from above relative to what has been written for these names. Do not interpret it as an oracle. Continue, asking simple yes or no, or give thanks and stop.

Second

This way requires you to read the signs named "Oracles."

You toss the coins asking a question about what you would like to know, or if you do not ask any question, it is what advice you would need to have at this time.

Proceed by tossing the first Oracle and writing it down. Then, toss the second oracle and write it down. Finally, toss the third oracle and writing it down.

When tossing the coins always remember to read the signs by looking at the objects from closest to you to furthest to you. Reading a 1 or 0, from bottom to top.

How to Interpret

The first oracle is the name of what you are living at the moment. The second and third sign is the direction in which to take the first sign. In essence, the conversation relative to the situations involving the first sign.

After reading the oracles you can ask simple "Yes" and "No" questions and answers to clarify your position relative to the oracles.

Once obtaining an oracle some will ask, "what do I do to better or support positive changes in my life, according to what I just read"" Advice – talk to a religious elder for recommendation or clarifications. This is a system for aspiring priest to obtain wisdom, practice, and guidance. This system along with the guidance of an elder will support positive communication with an elder, which can lead to positive spiritual growth and development.

Always close at the end, with giving thanks, for the communication. Also, if you get stuck, do not hesitate to obtain wisdom from a more experienced elder mentor, or guide; Many blessings to all, BabaSixto (IfaOdara) Aboru, Aboye, Aboshe-she.

Invocation Prayer

Hymn 15 (from the book on the Dead Sea Scrolls)

I thank Thee, O Lord, and nothing exists except by Thy will; none can consider [Thy deep secrets] or contemplate Thy [mysteries]. What then is man that is earth, that shaped [from clay] and return to the dust, that Thou shouldst gave him to understand such marvels and make knows to him the counsel of [Thy truth]? Clay and dust that I am, what can I devise unless Thou wish it, an1 what contrive unless Thou desire it? What strength shall I have1unless Thou keep me upright, and how shall I understand unless by (the spirits) which Thou hast shaped for me? What can I say unless Thou open my mouth and how can I answer unless Thou enlighten me? Behold, Thou art Prince of gods and King of majesties, Lord of all spirits, Ruler of all creatures; nothing is done without Thee, and nothing is known without Thy will. Beside Thee there is nothing, and nothing can compare with Thee is strength; in the presence of Thy glory there is nothing, and Thy might is without price. Who among Thy great and marvelous creature can stand in the presence of Thy glory? How then can, he who returns to his dust? For Thy glory's sake alone hast Thou made all these things.

Lucumi Mojuba Prayer: For those for follow for Ifa-Lucumi tradition, please obtain a Yoruba Mojuba prayer from one of your elders.

Example 1 (Business Question):
"Contractor xxxx, is he the correct contractor for restoration of properties back in my home country?"

First toss – 0000 – Oyekun – Eyioko – Cowrie (2)
2nd toss – 1100 – Eyeife – Iroso – Cowrie (4)
3rd toss – 0100 – Okana Sodde – Ika – Cowrie (14)

Note: Only pick out the information from the advices that are pertinent to the question or reason for doing the reading.

First cast Oyeku – so you look in the booklet and read Oyekun **"As an Oracle"**

"As an oracle it signifies the land of the dead mother earth. Where everything dies, decomposes, becomes nourishment for life to regenerate all over again. It is an oracle of materialism, abundance, being greedy, and change. It is to take care of yourself so that blessing is not short-living or fall apart in fron of you. It is an oracle of being indebted to the divinities. Promises must be kept there are unfinished , or undone spiritual labors/tasks that need to be completed before other changes can transpire. It is an oracle of knowing how to be obedient, listen and take advice, suffer the consequences of failure. **It means take your time and do the things right.** Oyekun is to never think you know more than the forces. It is one of adhering to the rules and hierarchy of divinities, spiritual, and physical (natural) worlds. Know your position, your role, and perform your duties as expected. It is an oracle of supporting, and expansion of family. **Know that your action can benefit**, as well as, hurt others, especially family."

Then, you toss two more times: and you read for those other two:

1100 – Eyeife – Iroso – Cowrie (4)

Iroso means the unknown, mysterious, occult, and surprises. It is to avoid entrapments or made part of grander scheme. Iroso has a saying, "Non one knows the mysteries which lie beneath the depths of the seas." As in a blessing, which can come out of nowhere; as well as trouble when taken in negative context. It is an oracle of discovery as much as it is of danger of business takeovers, being jacked, risky business, as it is of risk which lands a score, or jackpot. It makrs life coming to an end regarding a terminal illness. The person needs to work diligently with the divinities, Orisha, and ancestors to avoid accidents, fires, and diseases anything that can lead to shortening they stay here. **Advice: avoid crooked people, where people try to make a living out of illegal means –** "If you can't do the time – don't do the crime."

0100 – Okana Sodde – Ika – Cowrie (14)

Ika means to know how to get around situations, things, or finding your way. It is the need to obtain stability. If the individual has been thrown out, expelled, or lost their stability. They need to work diligently performing all necessary rituals or spiritual work to get to where they need to be. It is imperative that they find a new job, home, mater, or start over a family. **Ika is an oracle of a time of battle and the work that needs to be done to win. Ika is an oracle of going on the roads towards finding ones profession, city** or town where one is going to be successful. Where you are at the time might not be the correct place. This is why one is struggling so much. Not to get into a witchcraft war or power struggle with anyone.

You read the three and relate them to the question you asked. Them you get rid of any doubts in your interpretations by asking questions to obtain a direct "Yes" or "No" response. This is where you take the advice of the simple toss.

Interpretation:
Oyekun – It is good that you are doing things to help the land, yourself, and family.

Iroso – If the person is crooked and not trustworthy, then you can lose. If the person is good, then all things will be done well. Also, while you are not there, you will be taking a risk with whomever anyway.

Ika – Of the person you are asking about has no stability, has been fired or let go from their job, they need money. So, if the job is not being done, it is because they are using some of your money from their expenses. If they have money, they don't need your money, and the money you send will be allocated to the project.

Based on this you would ask – "Is the contractor a good contractor?
If yes, then does he need more money to do a good job?
If yes, once I give him more money will all renovations go according to plan?

If No, he's not a good contractor.
If No, once I give him more money the renovations won't get done?

Then, according to the signs, you have to find another contractor.

Example 2 (Relationship Question)
Question: "Does X person make a good romantic partner for me?"

First toss –   0101 – Eyeife – Ofun – Cowrie (10)
2nd toss –   1100 – Eyeife – Iroso – Cowrie (4)
3rd toss –   0101 – Eyeife – Ofun – Cowrie (10)

Toss 1: Main topic
0101 – Eyeife – Ofun – Cowrie (10)

Ofun is an oracle of self-defense, where defending yourself is permitted. It is an oracle of great wisdom, growth, and grandeur. Yet, not to allow the grandeur to get one's head, so as not to suffer failures. It is an oracles of perfection, and balance. Again like all greatness without humility, without understanding limitations, demine follows. It is the oracle of understanding death, and that all endings are a new beginning. What death represents, the land of the dead, working with the dead, elevation of the dead, ancestor worship. This oracle personifies living in harmony with society, nature, and your surroundings – Tao. It is where God's Messengers/ Holy Scriptures/ Word enters the world to teach mankind how to better live. Signifies losing one's life by overstepping one's position, disobedience, risk, or imposing will for selfish gain. What comes to mind with this oracle is "You're only as strong as the next person, who is equal to you or stronger."

Toss 2: Conversation relating to Main topic
1100 – Eyeife – Iroso – Cowrie (4)

Iroso means the unknown, mysterious, occult, and surprises. It is to avoid entrapments, or made part of grander scheme. Iroso has a saying, "No one knows the mysteries which lie beneath the depths of the seas." As in a blessing which can come out of nowhere, as well as, trouble when taken in negative context. It is an oracle of discovery as much as it of danger of business takeovers, being jacked, risky business, as it is risk which lands a score, or jackpot. It marks life coming to an end regarding a terminal illness. The person needs to work diligently with the divinities, Orisha, and ancestors to avoid accidents, fires, and diseases; anything that can lead to shortening their stay here. Advice: avoid crooked people, where people try to make a living out of illegal means – "If you can't do the time – don't do the crime."

Toss 3: Closing Argument or Outcome
0101 – Eyeife – Ofun – Cowrie (10)

Ofun is an oracle of self-defense, where defending yourself is permitted. It is an oracle of great wisdom, growth, and grandeur. Yet, not to allow the grandeur to get one's head, so as not to suffer failure. It is an oracle of perfection, and balance. Again like all greatness without humility, without understanding limitations demise follows. It is the oracles of understanding death, and that all endings are a new beginning.

What death represents, the land of the dead, working with the dead, elevation of the death, ancestor worship. This oracle personifies living in harmony with society, nature, and your surroundings – Tao. It is where God's Messengers/ Holy Scriptures/ Word enters the world to teach mankind how to better live. Signifies losing one's life by overstepping one's position, disobedience, risk, or imposing will for selfish gain. What comes to mind with this oracle is "You're only as strong as the next person, who is equal to you or stronger."

To summarize:

Ofun – Not to allow the relationship to go to one's head. To take a balanced approach to relationship. Harmonizing as getting to know how each other's lives, within society, and surrounding. Are you both ready to live together to see if you can harmonize, or take things slow?

Iroso – Still a realm of the unknown, yet open up so that there no mysteries in the relationship. What ever is hidden must come out. If there are still ties to an ex, all ties must be se11vered. Any court cases, or legal issues involved in, to always be clear. No surprises later as in "you never told me before." Discovery – you still need to learn more about each other. This is a fragile o1acles because anything wrong that one does or says to the other can cause the romance to die. It is always risky when one attempts to become romantically involved with another.

Ofun – Defend your position with reasons as to the whys? Relative to situation in your life (of course when in dialogue). In Ofun, each other's limitations are to be known. One is not to imposes impose will on the other. Both have to put in the time and effort to make the relationship a good at lasting lost.

Note: When reading as an oracle stay as an oracle and don't revert to reading the yes or no answers as in the first system. There are two systems here – the simple yes or no - or a more complex system by taking a simple yes or no and expanding it with one of the 16 geomancy codes. You must be careful not to lose or confuse yourself going back and forth between the two.

I-Ching Enhancement of Ifa 16 Oracle Divination System

By enhancing your Ifa 16 Oracle reading with an I Ching reading, you are partaking in a very complex divination that will further enhance the advice that you are seeking. You can utilize any I Ching book with interpretation preferences along with the geomancy tetragrams in this book. Included in this book are the Sixty-four I Ching Hexagrams with unique author interpretations along with one imbedded tetragram corresponding to both Pen-Kua, and Hu-Kua Hexagrams. The Tetragrams explanations are the same sixteen geomancy codes found in the beginning of the book. This book is designed to function with both systems independently, and as explained above enhancing one another.

Sharing this knowledge and writing this book has been a labor of love. I have been supporting the spiritual needs of countless individuals for a very long time, and during this practice I have encouraged folks to learn a divination system. A divination system serves as self-care, self-enlightenment, self-wisdom, and self-counsel methodology. When you can obtain answers from your spirituality, and proof of its truth. You are on the way towards making better choices and decisions, which lead to less mistakes and failures in life.

Part 2
I Chingmancy - 16 Oracle Ifa Codes with I Ching Enhancement

The Yoruba 16 Oracle Geomancy Codes with
I Ching Tetragram

Alafia - Simple Obi Toss all four up, 4 heads

Yes - thank you, health, and happiness; perfect answer when having placed an offering or libation to divinity and wishing to verify that it's been well received. When having asked a question, it's also interpreted as "Yes" thank you for asking. Alafia also represents wisdom and great spirituality, but most of all good health, and things being on the right path. Alafia is obtained when you are beginning an enterprise.

Alafia - In IFa Ogbe (1111) - Cowrie - Eyeunle (08) - I Ching Voyage (01)

1
1
1
1

I Ching tetragram 01 - Voyage; Yoruba Cowrie 08 - Eyeunle; Yoruba IFa Ogbe

Ogbe is the oracle of consciousness and will. So, you think so you are, where your mind takes you, so there will you be. From a positive point of view, it's where one becomes proud of one's achievements or how far one has come/traveled. It's to be on track with achieving goals and to see things through. On a negative thought, once you've felt that you've reached the top, then the worst that can happen is to suffer a fall or loss. This is an oracle of going through separations and adaptation to change; especially after making decisions that take you in the wrong direction. It advises not to lose your head i.e., give in to negative ego, or impulses. It recommends patience and protective actions. If your time is up where you are, then it's time to move on; life is not just one journey, but a long road that never ends. Speaking in this oracle are all situations dealing with the mind, thoughts, knowledge, understanding, wisdom, and ignorance. Not thinking properly will lead to confrontations, and one must beware of never overstepping boundaries. Support unity, but if needing to separate do so without violence. Know that all endings lead to new beginnings. Beware of actions that can turn into a justice situation, or lawsuit. But most of all to be organized or bringing order to your life. This is an oracle of being saved by taking a leap of faith and entering some form of spiritual practice. Ogbe is also, road, path, and to be elevated to a new position. There is a tendency towards being or becoming narcissistic, selfish, and not empathic to others, i.e., arrogance and ignorance can lead to this. In essence, not to see through the eyes of others, or feel their concerns. It's not all about you, you affect others, and others you. Having bad behavior is imposing one's will to the extreme of not caring who they step on or who they injure along the way. It's there way or the highway; consequences to actions is sometimes overlooked when it comes to obtaining their means. One must be careful to bite more than one can chew. Things done by force will be met with contention and conflicts will follow. This is a mighty oracle announces blessings and successes that are to be achieved in ones' life. But, only through intelligence, wisdom, patience, and honorable means. All that can be supported by the will of God, and positive divinities in the right way.

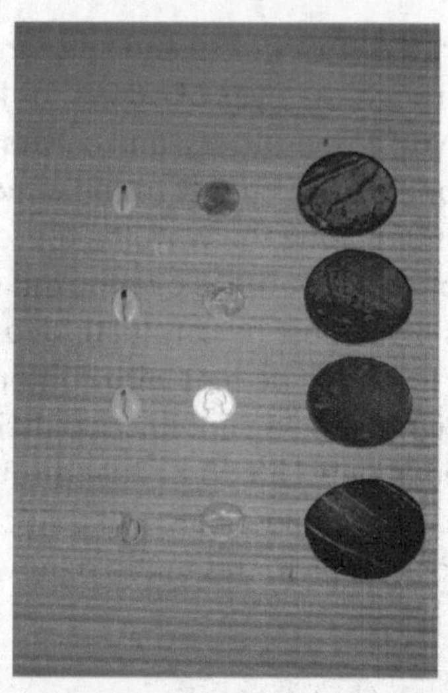

Itawa - Simple Obi Toss; three up one down; 3 heads and 1 tail

Almost - "Yes" or "Maybe" a subsequent toss is merited to obtain an Alafia, Eyeife, Okana Sorde, Okana Yekun, or another Itawa. Itawa has a saying, "Why ask what you already know?" Itawa also says, "It's perfect to know that there's nothing perfect, that's why it's perfect." Itawa regarding ritual is obtained when divinity is accepting the work being done, although it could have been done with more accuracy, detail, or better organization or substances. It's a sign of work to be continued as in it's not over yet. Itawa indicates follow up work needed to assure things go in the correct direction. There might be other divinities that would like to contribute to the success of the work being done. This is a sign that requires follow up and continued work. Itawa is work in progress.

Itawa's are: In IFa (**Ogunda**, Osa, Otura, & Irete); Cowrie (**03**, 09, 13, 16); I Ching (**Corruption**, Rising, Activities, and Grace)

1
1
1
0

I Ching tetragram 02 - Corruption; Yoruba Cowrie 03 - Ogunda; Yoruba IFa Ogunda

This is an oracle of being dedicated to a profession, as well as safeguarding your position, title, work, or livelihood. It's to avoid putting your freedom at risk i.e., justice situation. Avoid putting your life at risk through physical altercations, or quarreling. It's an oracle of fights, violence, stealing, or desiring a big score; in essence, beware of desiring to obtain things through force or illegal means. Never take advantage of the weak, mistreat others, or you'll suffer being mistreated. Someone needs protection against justice situations or help in winning a court case, or battle in general. Beware of injury working with tools, vehicles, accidents due to stress or over working. Oracle of having strength but knowing when and how to use it. Wasted strength depletes and turns into a weakness. One needs to be tenderer and earn the respect of mates and others through kindness. Ogunda teaches us that war is necessary for peace to reign in the end. But everything doesn't have to be a battle when you can win with wisdom. The greatest asset of Ogunda is to become educated, acquiring skills, or recognizing one's talent and profiting from it. This is an oracle of creating, inventing, constructing, building, and engineering. Learn, especially about what tools you will need that can support your talents or make your life easier. Oracle of work, and making oneself useful, not useless.

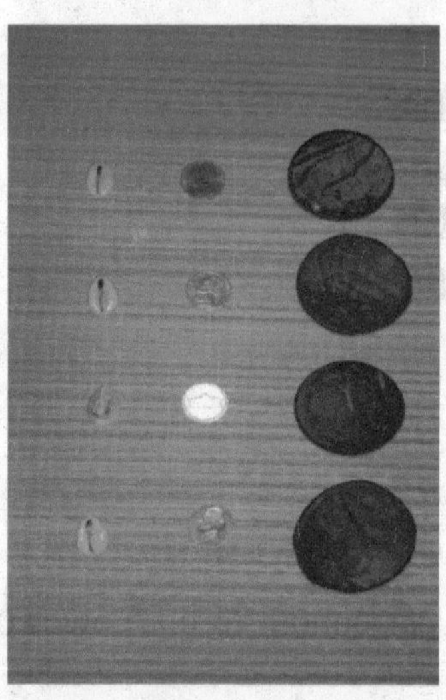

Itawa - Simple Obi Toss; three up one down; 3 heads and 1 tail

Almost - "Yes" or "Maybe" a subsequent toss is merited to obtain an Alafia, Eyeife, Okana Sorde, Okana Yekun, or another Itawa. Itawa has a saying, "Why ask what you already know?" Itawa also says, "It's perfect to know that there's nothing perfect, that's why it's perfect." Itawa regarding ritual is obtained when divinity is accepting the work being done, although it could have been done with more accuracy, detail, or better organization or substances. It's a sign of work to be continued as in it's not over yet. Itawa indicates follow up work needed to assure things go in the correct direction. There might be other divinities that would like to contribute to the success of the work being done. This is a sign that requires follow up and continued work. Itawa is work in progress.

Itawa's are: In IFa (Ogunda, Osa, Otura, **& Irete**); Cowrie (3, 9, **13**, 16); I Ching (Corruption, Rising, **Activities**, and Grace)

1
1
0
1

I Ching tetragram 03 - Activities; Yoruba Cowrie 13 - Metanla; Yoruba IFa Irete

Irete is an oracle of being sought after looked for or found. Beware of investigations, or being probed, and getting caught. Irete represents escaping, an escape, climbing out of a hole/ditch, or getting out of a rut. When desperate or in despair there will be someone or a situation will arise that will give way to the needed support in overcoming the difficulty. Irete is an oracle of upward mobility as in stepping up a ladder or striving towards bettering oneself, rising above the rest, or rising to the occasion. It is one of undergoing physical challenges, beware of early disease or injuries to one's limbs via falling and fracturing. Also beware of accidents, not being mindful. When it comes to women this is a sign that relates to difficult pregnancies. In general, beware of love triangles and promiscuity, which can lead to STDs. Learning how to attend to spirit guides and ancestors is important because it's a sign that marks communications with them. Learn to be obedient and listen to ancestral advice. There will be a reunion or gathering soon. The person needs much love, romanticism, and finding the correct mate to ensure happiness. This is not something that happens trying too hard. It's something the happens being at the right place and right time. In Irete religious activities are much more favorable to the person's energy than social ones (partying).

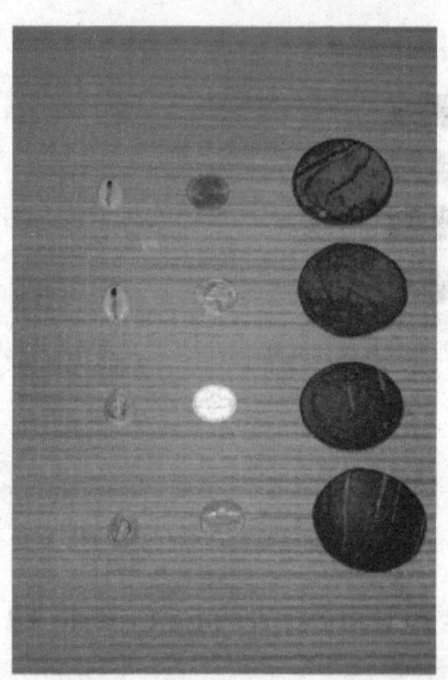

Eyeife – Simple Obi Toss – two up two down; two heads and two tails

"Yes," affirmative, all will be resolved. The work being done is correct and exact. Also, a good outcome to situations sought. Differs from the Alafia's "Yes," which in comparison demands correct action to not loose blessings. Differs from Itawa's "Yes," where it is work in progress and follows up with more work. Eyeife shows things coming to pass. It's coming to the completion of efforts taken in resolve. Itawa's come before Eyeife as indicators of resolve. Alafia's come after Eyeife, in appreciation of having faith in the divinities. Eyeife is to be on track with meeting one's objective.

Eyeife's are in IFa – (Iwori, Odi, **Iroso**, Ojuani, Oche, Ofun); Cowrie (15, 07, **04**, 11, 05, 10).
In I Ching (Agreements, Obstacles, **Enthusiasm,** Success, Dissolution, & Limitations)

1
1
0
0

I Ching tetragram 03 - Enthusiasm; Yoruba Cowrie 04 - Iroso; Yoruba IFa Iroso

Iroso means the unknown, mysterious, hidden, secrets, and surprises. 11This is a sign of riches, obtaining, inheriting, or achieving status. It's to avoid entrapments of being made part of a grander scheme. Iroso has a saying, "No one knows the mysteries that lie beneath the depths of the seas." As in a blessing, which can come out of nowhere; as well as trouble when taken in a negative context. It's an oracle of discovery as much as it is of exposure to danger. It announces a business takeover or being taken advantage of. It recommends avoiding risky business to minimize losses or ending up catching a court case. It marks life coming to an end regarding a terminal illness or having a short life due to lifestyle choices. The person needs to work diligently with the divinities and ancestors to avoid anger issues, heart disease, or other sudden incidentals due to living a stressful life. This is an oracle of avoiding being crooked or influenced by criminal elements or intentions. Iroso is an oracle of traps being laid, hidden agendas, extortion, or blackmail. "If you can't do the time, then don't do the crime." If you like an adrenaline rush and exposing yourself and others to danger, then be ready to pay for the consequences of those actions. Beware of someone desiring to get rid of you from somewhere, removing, or getting you out of the way for them to take over. Oracle of being let go, fired or no longer desired.

Itawa - Simple Obi Toss; three up one down; 3 heads and 1 tail

Almost - "Yes" or "Maybe" a subsequent toss is merited to obtain an Alafia, Eyeife, Okana Sorde, Okana Yekun, or another Itawa. Itawa has a saying, "Why ask what you already know?" Itawa also says, "It's perfect to know that there's nothing perfect, that's why it's perfect." Itawa regarding ritual is obtained when divinity is accepting the work being done, although it could have been done with more accuracy, detail, or better organization or substances. It's a sign of work to be continued as in it's not over yet. Itawa indicates follow up work needed to assure things go in the correct direction. There might be other divinities that would like to contribute to the success of the work being done. This is a sign that requires follow up and continued work. Itawa is work in progress.

Itawa's are: In IFa (Ogunda, Osa, **Otura**, & Irete); Cowrie (3, 9, 13, **16**); I Ching (Corruption, Rising, Activities, and **Grace**)

1
0
1
1

I Ching tetragram 05 - Grace; Yoruba Cowrie 16 - Meridilogun; Yoruba IFa Otura

Otura speaks of living in an inhospitable place. It's to be surrounded or live among con artists, and thieves. Also, to avoid being conned or tricked, someone is to be outwitted. Never be the first to know or know the most and the last to take advantage of opportunities. This is a sign of not being given recognition for your efforts or taken for granted. Don't take things for granted, life, family, relationship, jobs, or career, etc. Oracle of being too slow to take advantage of an opportunity due to being distracted. The person needs to have a sharp mind and keep things in order. Not saying you are going to do but doing it, especially with honor. The sooner an individual acquires the necessary skills, and identifies their talents or career, the sooner they will be successful. Oracle prescribes not allowing situations to drag. Bringing closure to situations will allow for one to go on to the next thing without skipping a beat. This sign doesn't permit delaying because carelessness and making mistakes will take hold. Oracle of knowing how to live within your means, respect, and worships the forces of God. How well and proficient individual works with the divine forces, so will their grace bring them blessings. Speaks of dark forces robbing the person's luck, happiness, and economic well-being when not appeased or expunged in time. Yet, Otura is an oracle of resolving with good luck when situations are taken care of in time. Identify grace, gift, or being gracious in doing things with good taste, will win the hearts of others. And, with this comes the necessary support, not being alone, or left alone with all the weight upon your shoulders.

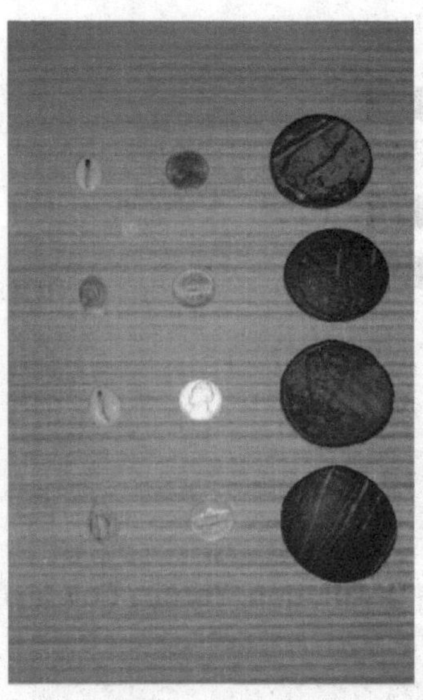

Eyeife – Simple Obi Toss – two up two down; two heads and two tails

"Yes," affirmative, all will be resolved. The work being done is correct and exact. Also, a good outcome to situations sought. Differs from the Alafia's "Yes," which in comparison demands correct action to not loose blessings. Differs from Itawa's "Yes," where it is work in progress and follows up with more work. Eyeife shows things coming to pass. It's coming to the completion of efforts taken in resolve. Itawa's come before Eyeife as indicators of resolve. Alafia's come after Eyeife, in appreciation of having faith in the divinities. Eyeife is to be on track with meeting one's objective.

Eyeife's are in IFa – (Iwori, Odi, Iroso, Ojuani, **Oche**, Ofun); Cowrie (15, 07, 04, 11, **05**, 10).
In I Ching (Agreements, Obstacles, Enthusiasm, Success, **Dissolution**, & Limitations)

1
0
1
0

I Ching tetragram 06 - Dissolution; Yoruba Cowrie 05 - Oche; Yoruba IFa Oche

Oracle of the blood being thicker than water, blood being the transporter of cells for living organisms to function. In essence, blood is life. Oracle where money came into the world, and today is the lifeblood of society, business, commerce, or government economies. This is an oracle of fights over money, and in some cases over livelihood (bringing food to your table). Oracle of being cheated or feeling cheated. It's the oracle where the money is cursed, or "the root to all evil." Human blood feeds money i.e., the blood sweat, and tears of those that work to survive. Rich folks curse it because many of them don't want to lose it. Poor folks curse it because they don't have it, and it eludes them. In Oche negativity stems from the decomposition of things, corruption, failures, when situations fall apart. Uncleanliness, impurities, or filthiness corrupts and generates diseases. Hence, sanitize, wash, purify, and never allow germs, parasites, or viruses to take hold. Taking care of one's digestion, and blood is important to avoid illnesses or diseases from an early age. Oche is an oracle of dysfunctional, disorganized family, relationships, or affairs. The protection of the family, economic position, and not allowing for relationship problems getting in the way of happiness is key to being successful. In this oracle one is to make one's spirituality stronger through dedication, devotion, and being responsible with one's gift; otherwise, one loses the gift and gives way to the decomposition of all things. Oche is an oracle of protecting that which you've worked so hard to maintain. Love God and his divinities so you attend them, so will they support you in getting out of situations and resolving for better living. Oche is an oracle of needing to be saved through taking a leap of faith and entering a shamanistic priestly way of life.

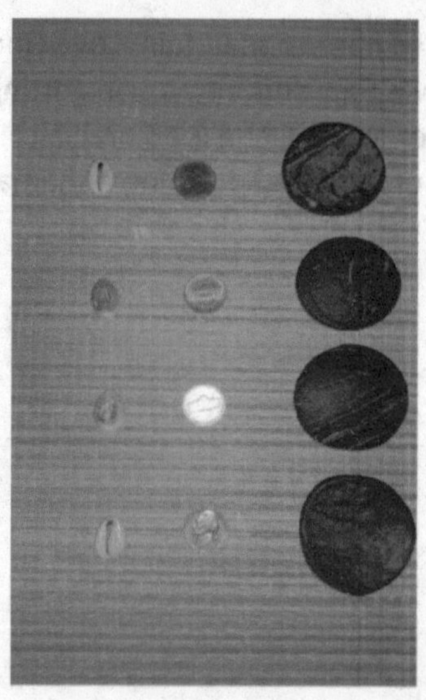

Eyeife – Simple Obi Toss – two up two down; two heads and two tails

"Yes," affirmative, all will be resolved. The work being done is correct and exact. Also, a good outcome to situations sought. Differs from the Alafia's "Yes," which in comparison demands correct action to not loose blessings. Differs from Itawa's "Yes," where it is work in progress and follows up with more work. Eyeife shows things coming to pass. It's coming to the completion of efforts taken in resolve. Itawa's come before Eyeife as indicators of resolve. Alafia's come after Eyeife, in appreciation of having faith in the divinities. Eyeife is to be on track with meeting one's objective.

Eyeife's are in IFa – (Iwori, **Odi**, Iroso, Ojuani, Oche, Ofun); Cowrie (15, **07**, 04, 11, 05, 10).
In I Ching (Agreements, **Obstacles**, Enthusiasm, Success, Dissolution, & Limitations)

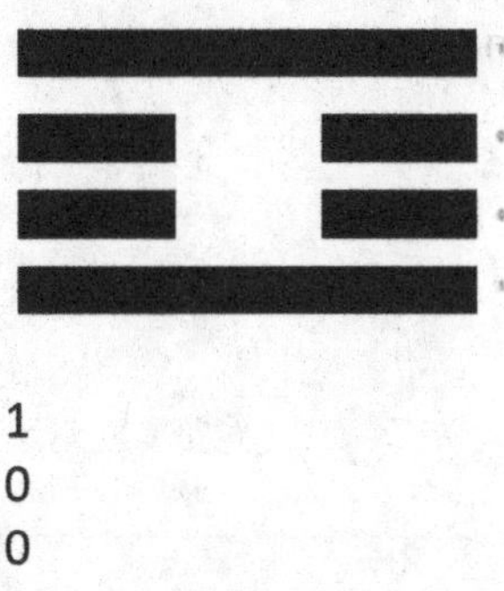

1
0
0
1

I Ching tetragram 07 - Obstacles; Yoruba Cowrie 07 - Odi; Yoruba IFa Odi

Odi is an oracle of great luck, and of having strong spirit guides, and ancestor links that when used properly and developed will bring about great things to a person's life. Oracle of individuals that can be a bit obnoxious overbearing or surrounded by obnoxious overbearing people and situations. The greatest downfall in the person's life according to this oracle is gossip, being nosy, and false witnessing. Also, speaking out of context, or giving out information to the wrong individuals at the wrong time. It's an oracle of having some sort of habit or addiction, i.e., an addictive personality. Substances abuse situations will lead to the destruction not only of the person's organism but of others and all happiness around them. Speaks of the creation of the marketplace learning sales, money management, having own business, or running someone's business. Oracle of feminism, and the gift of being a woman in bringing forth life into the world. The individual must be more objective, toughen their heart, and control emotions. Because this oracle is of being emotional, or emotional situations being hard for the person to handle. Keeping a marriage will be a challenge and difficult due to emotional imbalances, jealousy issues, pride, ego, or constantly picking the wrong individual. Speaks of suffering childhood traumas that still affect the individual even throughout adulthood. Getting along with one's family can be difficult. Oracle where family members become enemies of one another. Ancestors demand family unity. Avoid indecisiveness, selfishness, and promiscuity. Oracle of a hole, crater, ditch, crevasse, or grave. Advice is to not make decisions or make lifestyle choices that lead to an early grave, for many pitfalls.

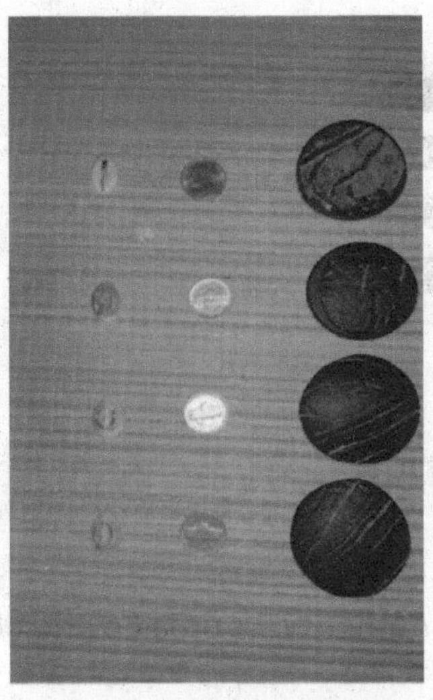

Okana Sodde - Simple Obi Toss - three down, one up; 3 tails 1 head

A straight "No," - don't, not this, something else and stop - check on something else desired at the time, or something is not correct 11at the time according to what you are asking... Many don't like to receive a "No" when asking or performing ritual work, yet how can divinities tell you what to change or switch with a "Yes." So, the "No" is a good indicator of the divinities communicating with you and specifying how they want things done. It's not always that "No" means not to do something, it can also mean stop change the order of things or find the best path. "No" can also mean it is not the proper time for obtaining desires, energies in your surroundings are not positively aligned, or conducive to favoring your actions at this moment. Also, there may be other rituals or much more work needed to be done for a positive outcome. With tossing an Itawa before followed by an Okana, it's obvious that it means "Maybe + No" ask for something else, in another way, or something is missing, there's a need to add more things – things are unsure.

Okana Sodde's are in IFa (Okana, **Obara**, Ika, Otrupon; Cowrie 01, **06**, 12, 14; I Ching (Failure, **Authority**, Peace, & Violation)

1
0
0
0

I Ching tetragram 08 - Authority; Yoruba Cowrie 06 - Obara; Yoruba IFa Obara

Obara says, "There can't be changed without revolution - chaos or torment." An oracle of wisdom, intelligence, and learning how to better live or coexist with those in your environment. Business related relative to marketing and knowing how to deliver goods to markets. The market rises, and the markets fall. It's where wheels turn/move forward, but there are times when we need to turn back or go backwards. Obara is an oracle where being proud leads to starvation, being left alone, or being put to the side. Oracle of success or failure, where the tongue, verb, or speaking can save you or do you in. The tongue can be used for evil, as it can be used for good. Good when it's used to praise, pray for good things, and bless. Evil went it's used to offend, false witness, and lie. So, mind your tongue. Speaks of knowing how to stay standing up and not falling after having worked hard in obtaining a position or move up in life. Speaks of good business relations when fair. Speaks of difficulties in maintaining relationships (personal, social) due to being difficult to satisfy. In Obara one needs to maintain focus on education and utilizing one's talents or gifts to become successful. One is not to allow matters of the heart, emotions, or promiscuity to get in the way of one's success. Concentration and focus on achievements will bring happiness and many positive things. Giving in to pettiness, childishness, egotism, and distractions will lead to failure. The individual from a young age must learn to discern lies, and not fall into anti-social behavior. This will inevitably lead to doom. This is an oracle of planning, setting goals, and knowing how to execute the plan. Oracle of conquering and escaping danger when knowing how n1ot to be in the wrong place, and at the wrong time. This is an oracle of not being a liar, learning that there is no honor in lying.

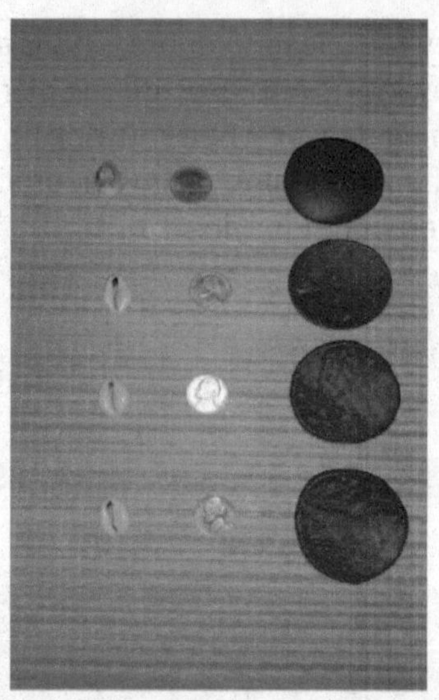

Itawa - Simple Obi Toss; three up one down; 3 heads and 1 tail

Almost - "Yes" or "Maybe" a subsequent toss is merited to obtain an Alafia, Eyeife, Okana Sorde, Okana Yekun, or another Itawa. Itawa has a saying, "Why ask what you already know?" Itawa also says, "It's perfect to know that there's nothing perfect, that's why it's perfect." Itawa regarding ritual is obtained when divinity is accepting the work being done, although it could have been done with more accuracy, detail, or better organization or substances. It's a sign of work to be continued as in it's not over yet. Itawa indicates follow up work needed to assure things go in the correct direction. There might be other divinities that would like to contribute to the success of the work being done. This is a sign that requires follow up and continued work. Itawa is work in progress.

Itawa's are: In IFa (Ogunda, **Osa**, Otura, & Irete); Cowrie (03, **09**, 13, 16); I Ching (Corruption, **Rising**, Activities, and Grace)

0
1
1
1

I Ching tetragram 09 - Rising; Yoruba Cowrie 09 - Osa; Yoruba IFa Osa

Osa is an oracle that signifies things being up in the air. Up for grabs, unsure, or insecure. Religious and spiritual work may support and solidify marriage, job, health, and family situations. But not all situations can be manipulated or resolved through ritual work, or spiritual practices. There is also common sense, logic, and facing reality. We can be our own worst enemy when being willful, selfish, and wanting things our way despite the greater good of things around us. In essence, never to give in, to selfishness. Obstacles occur due to not giving what is necessary to the divinities in time. All divinities and forces merit their fair share of attention. Spirit guides and ancestors need to be given light, especially those, which have died tragically or recently. Oracle of understanding the spiritual ideology of giving light, obtaining enlightenment, and finding one's spiritual purpose. Prescribes coming out of the dark and opening one's eyes to the truth. Some only believe their truth, never mind common sense, logic, and the obvious. Oracle of not living in denial, especially when things are staring you in the face. Beware of hiding behind pretenses as a way of feeling empowered. Osa is also, an oracle of understanding investments, finances, and money matters. Never try to get over on others or earn a living through taking advantage of people. What goes around comes around. Not being cheap, yet conscientious, and sharing with others will always return benefits. This is an oracle of staying consistent in one's investments, businesses in the time will get better. Fast money doesn't last long, money earned throughout a period is much more profitable. not giving up. If money is not managed properly, you are sure to struggle. Osa is also an oracle of understanding female contribution in all things. It is one of understanding the feminine temperament and when the female energy is an asset. But also, beware of imbalances that cause this energy to become erratic. Osa is an oracle of getting along with others, and all people in general.

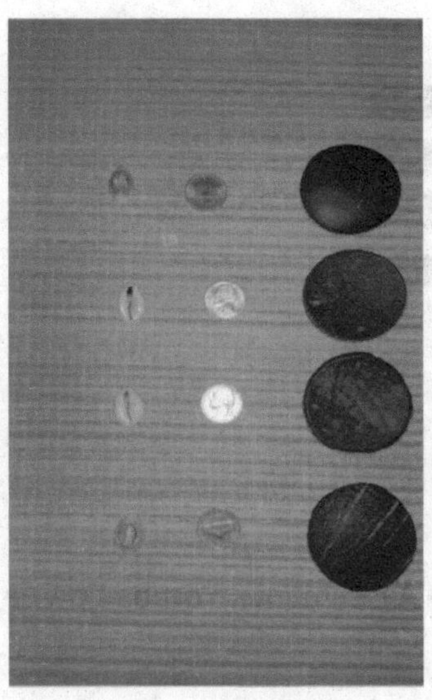

Eyeife – Simple Obi Toss – two up two down; two heads and two tails

"Yes," affirmative, all will be resolved. The work being done is correct and exact. Also, a good outcome to situations sought. Differs from the Alafia's "Yes," which in comparison demands correct action to not loose blessings. Differs from Itawa's "Yes," where it is work in progress and follows up with more work. Eyeife shows things coming to pass. It's coming to the completion of efforts taken in resolve. Itawa's come before Eyeife as indicators of resolve. Alafia's come after Eyeife, in appreciation of having faith in the divinities. Eyeife is to be on track with meeting one's objective.

Eyeife's are in IFa – (**Iwori**, Odi, Iroso, Ojuani, Oche, Ofun); Cowrie (**15**, 07, 04, 11, 05, 10).
In I Ching (**Agreements**, Obstacles, Enthusiasm, Success, Dissolution, & Limitations)

0
1
1
0

I Ching tetragram 10 - Agreements; Yoruba Cowrie 15 - Marunla; Yoruba IFa Iwori

Iwori is the oracle of your head's view on things or your head getting around to the right thought processes. It is to know what it means to think; think goodness as much as to know what it is to think evil and be evil. Oracle of never thinking one is a know it all, or to believe they know more than God, his divinities, and the land of the dead. It's the oracle of scientific discovery, technology, psychology, and all-around wisdom. Yet, maintaining a level head being constructive and not destructive. Beware of a mental breakdown due to overexerting one's brain in trying too hard to accomplish desires. It is wisdom to know that what is meant for you comes with little effort. Because it is meant be and easy, it is right and the right timing too. What is not meant is known because of the struggle that it takes trying to obtain it, only to lose it because it was not meant to be. The individual must beware of becoming overbearing, autocratic, or tyrannical because one will end up alone. Where privileged individuals can lose everything being overconfident, and making willful mistakes, they need to listen to others too and respect their advice or opinion. The greatest challenge is to learn how to obtain things by the grace of God, and divinities, not thinking all things come just because of your efforts. This demands great patience and allowing the divinities to bring things to you. Iwori's inner or external battle relates to finding their right place in the world. Frustration can come from the inability to uphold a position in society that is recognizable. They have a great need to feel that they are not just contributing to family, community, or society but also leaving a mark. Iwori is an oracle where families destroy one another through infighting, competing, and showing who's the dominate one. Yet, they as a unit become a force to be reckoned with when united or focus on the greater good of the whole family. Individuals should work on forging a legacy that lasts generations in this way they will truly make their mark on life.

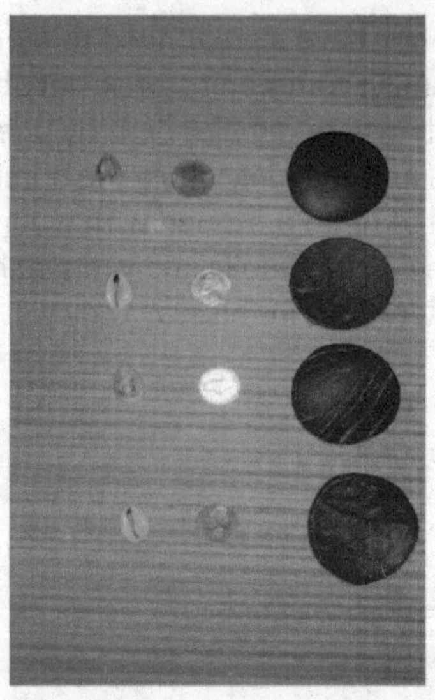

Eyeife – Simple Obi Toss – two up two down; two heads and two tails

"Yes," affirmative, all will be resolved. The work being done is correct and exact. Also, a good outcome to situations sought. Differs from the Alafia's "Yes," which in comparison demands correct action to not loose blessings. Differs from Itawa's "Yes," where it is work in progress and follows up with more work. Eyeife shows things coming to pass. It's coming to the completion of efforts taken in resolve. Itawa's come before Eyeife as indicators of resolve. Alafia's come after Eyeife, in appreciation of having faith in the divinities. Eyeife is to be on track with meeting one's objective.

Eyeife's are in IFa – (Iwori, Odi, Iroso, Ojuani, Oche, **Ofun**); Cowrie (15, 07, 04, 11, 05, **10**). In I Ching (Agreements, Obstacles, Enthusiasm, Success, Dissolution, & **Limitations**)

0
1
0
1

I Ching tetragram 11 - Limitations; Yoruba Cowrie 10 - Ofun; Yoruba IFa Ofun

Ofun is an oracle of self-defense, where defending yourself is permitted. It's an oracle of great wisdom, growth, and grandeur. Yet, not to allow the grandeur to get one's head, or it will cause failures and setbacks. This oracle stresses seeking perfection and balance. In essence, greatness without humility or not knowing limitations will lead to demise and destruction. This oracle personifies living in harmony with society, nature, and your surroundings - Tao. It's where God's messengers/holy scriptures/words and testaments enter the world to teach mankind how to better live. Signifies losing one's life accidentally, or by mistake. Oracle recommends never overstepping one's position, being disobedient, taking unnecessary risk, or imposing will on others. This is an oracle of understanding boundaries, limitations, and knowing which lines are never too cross. What comes to mind with this oracle is "You're only as strong as the next person, which is equal to you or stronger." Ofun is an oracle of recognizing we can't know everything; we can't have everything, and we will lose thinking we are everything. Beware of stepping out of line with one's actions or misjudging individuals. Oracle of being mindful of one's actions and the consequences that they can cause, as well as the actions of others along the same lines. With this oracle we learn to understand the nature of death. As in the cycle of a disease individual that slowly deteriorates leading to death. This cycle includes the individual and family coping with the process, beginning with denial, anger, anxiety, depression, acceptance, and finally grief. The spiritual process begins with death (reapers) coming to meet, hopefully in a controlled way, but as we know death can be sudden too. Then, the crossing over, extends to family acknowledging their ancestors, and initiating spiritual practices for the transcendence of their souls. Ofun represents processes involving the land of the dead, working with the dead, elevation or crossing over of the dead through ancestor worship.

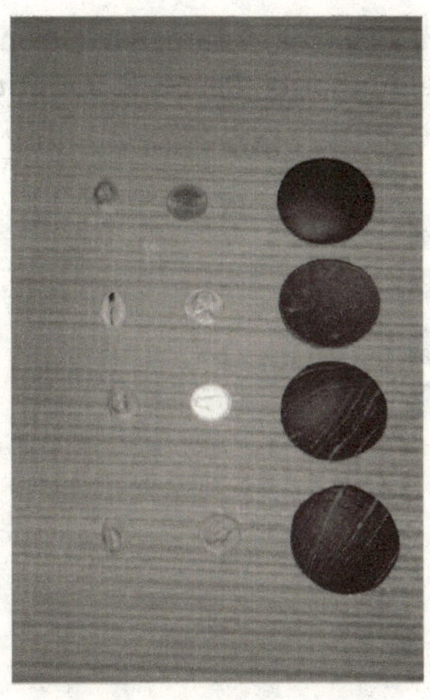

Okana Sodde - Simple Obi Toss - three down, one up; 3 tails 1 head

A straight "No," - don't, not this, something else and stop - check on something else desired at the time, or something is not correct at the time according to what you are asking... Many don't like to receive a "No" when asking or performing ritual work, yet how can divinities tell you what to change or switch with a "Yes." So, the "No" is a good indicator of the divinities communicating with you and specifying how they want things done. It's not always that "No" means not to do something, it can also mean stop change the order of things or find the best path. "No" can also mean it is not the proper time for obtaining desires, energies in your surroundings are not positively aligned, or conducive to favoring your actions at this moment. Also, there may be other rituals or much more work needed to be done for a positive outcome. With tossing an Itawa before followed by an Okana, it's obvious that it means "Maybe + No" ask for something else, in another way, or something is missing, there's a need to add more things – things are unsure.

Okana Sodde's are in IFa (Okana, Obara, **Ika**, Otrupon; Cowrie 01, 06, 12, **14**; I Ching (Failure, Authority, Peace, & **Violation**)

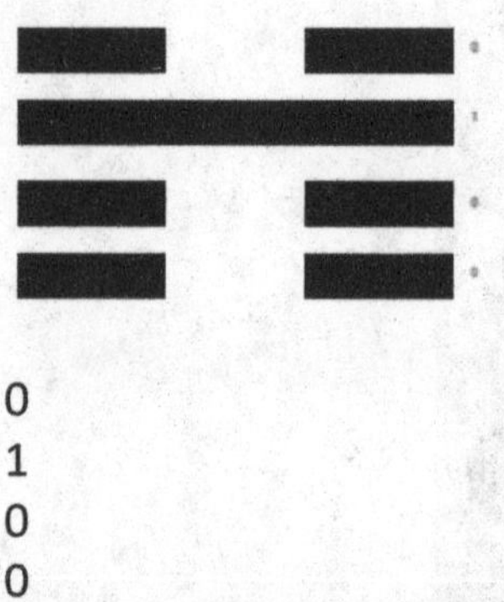

0
1
0
0

I Ching tetragram 12 - Violation; Yoruba Cowrie 14 - Merinla; Yoruba IFa Ika

Ika means to know how to get around situations. It is an oracle of finding the correct approach to things. One needs to find themselves, and their correct way of being. But most importantly stability in life, i.e., where or what brings stability. If the individual has been kicked out, lost their job/home, their stability? They will need to help in getting back on track. Look to spirituality for this support or find those that can give guidance and ritual work to bring you back from the loss. Ika is an oracle of going to battle, or having to battle, along with the work that is needed to win. It's where we as young folks hit the road of life in a direction towards finding our profession, place, position, where one is going to be successful. If you find yourself struggling to much and going through obstacles and hard times. This is a definite indicator that you are not where you need to be. Ika is an oracle of avoiding battles or getting out them. Avoid spiritual battles with folks that utilize spirituality to do harm. Suggest too, allow elders or more experienced people to help you through guidance; don't try to be a know it all. Ika is an oracle of helping others and through goodwill unto others, returning favors or someone least expected help you when most needed occurs. Hence, one is not to reject help due to pride. This is an oracle of the family not harming one another. Beware of being kicked out your home, job, work, relationship, or someplace due to not recognizing what's been going on. In essence you snooze you lose. Oracle of understanding what is evident or inevitable. Understand that most situations can be resolved just by getting out of the way or addressing issues in time.

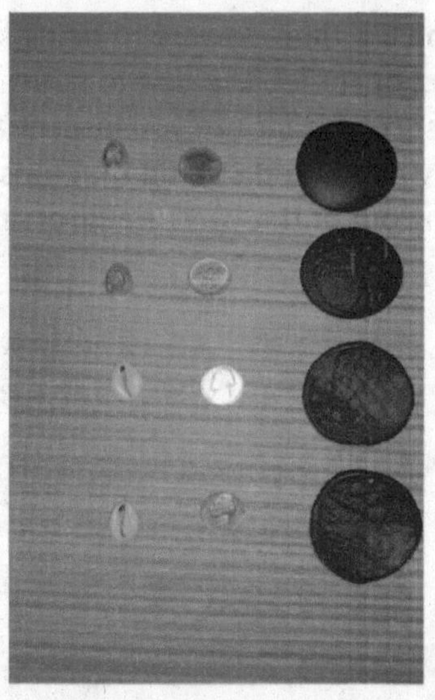

Eyeife – Simple Obi Toss – two up two down; two heads and two tails

"Yes," affirmative, all will be resolved. The work being done is correct and exact. Also, a good outcome to situations sought. Differs from the Alafia's "Yes," which in comparison demands correct action to not loose blessings. Differs from Itawa's "Yes," where it is work in progress and follows up with more work. Eyeife shows things coming to pass. It's coming to the completion of efforts taken in resolve. Itawa's come before Eyeife as indicators of resolve. Alafia's come after Eyeife, in appreciation of having faith in the divinities. Eyeife is to be on track with meeting one's objective.

Eyeife's are in IFa – (Iwori, Odi, Iroso, **Ojuani**, Oche, Ofun); Cowrie (15, 07, 04, **11**, 05, 10). In I Ching (Agreements, Obstacles, Enthusiasm, **Success**, Dissolution, & Limitations)

0
0
1
1

I Ching tetragram 13 - Success; Yoruba Cowrie 11 - Ojuani; Yoruba IFa Ojuani

Ojuani means from riches to rags, and from rags to riches. It's an oracle of doubts, complexes, and potential insecurities. Persons have an overzealous ambition that when not held back can become destructive. Oracle where person's must keep their ego in check. Learn to live with others in peace strive for an education obtaining a career profession, or title. To be a responsible and not a careless individual, beware of desires; we can't have everything or everything we think is good for us might not be. Oracle of becoming easily bored with mates, so beware of promiscuity and STDs. People lose due to jealousy, and envy within a circle of friendships, work, and even family. Speaks of dark forces getting in the way of progress, external or internal. Oracle marks needing to be exorcised of dark energies/forces when prevalent i.e., noticed through not sleeping well, feeling haunted, or energy being sucked out of you. Beware of people that cling to you and become like a parasite, just as you should not be a parasite to anyone. Being sucked dry is noticed by how much you're losing due to relationship/business; not just money but also one's peace of mind, tranquility, or space. In this oracle, one's family or mate's family can be your worst enemy or the biggest asset depending on how much they care about you or love you. Oracle of hurting or injuring the one we love through our actions or not noticing that one is doing this. Beware of being head-strung and willful as in my way or the highway. One must be flexible or understand when one has encountered inflexible individuals that don't contribute to positive things but get in the way and disrupt one's happiness. Beware of justice situations through being involved with people that are into illegal activities. Beware of becoming involved in illegal activities due to not acquiring a career in time. Oracle of never being envious of others, oracle of knowing who's on your side, and not damaging relationships.

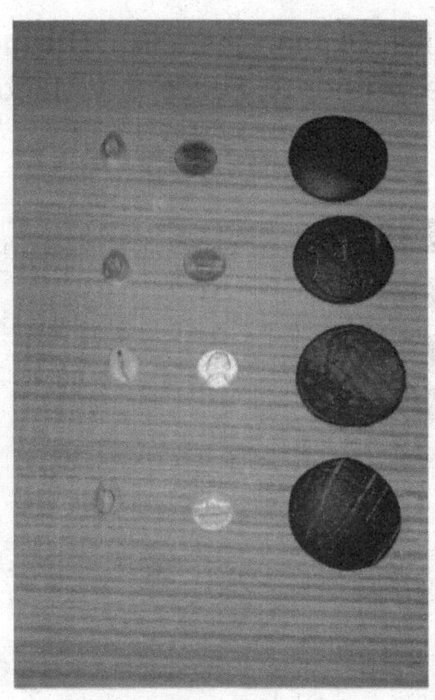

Okana Sodde - Simple Obi Toss - three down, one up; 3 tails 1 head

A straight "No," - don't, not this, something else and stop - check on something else desired at the time, or something is not correct at the time according to what you are asking... Many don't like to receive a "No" when asking or performing ritual work, yet how can divinities tell you what to change or switch with a "Yes." So, the "No" is a good indicator of the divinities communicating with you and specifying how they want things done. It's not always that "No" means not to do something, it can also mean stop change the order of things or find the best path. "No" can also mean it is not the proper time for obtaining desires, energies in your surroundings are not positively aligned, or conducive to favoring your actions at this moment. Also, there may be other rituals or much more work needed to be done for a positive outcome. With tossing an Itawa before followed by an Okana, it's obvious that it means "Maybe + No" ask for something else, in another way, or something is missing, there's a need to add more things – things are unsure.

Okana Sodde's are in IFa (Okana, Obara, Ika, **Otrupon**; Cowrie 01, 06, **12**, 14; I Ching (Failure, Authority, **Peace**, & Violation)

0
0
1
0

I Ching tetragram 14 - Purity; Yoruba Cowrie 12 - Eyila; Yoruba IFa Otrupon

Otrupon is to be offended, to offend, or someone is on the offensive. Implying the need to protect yourself. This is an oracle of overcoming traumas; bullied, violated, disrespected, embarrassed, harassed, assaulted, cursed out, or abused. Speaks of wanting out of a relation, situation, job, and unable to find the way out. There is someone that wants to take over or win everything at all costs. They would do whatever it takes to get someone out of their way and obtain their means. Not to give in to selfishness, ego, or pride; also, to never be prejudice, misjudge, nor persecute anyone unjustly. Speaks of family betraying one another. Where mates in a separation battle over possessions and custody to the brinks of destroying one another. After a storm comes to calm as in - we need to weather storms; know how to outlive ordeals. Otrupon is an oracle of peace and harmony returning after having undergone situations of great turmoil and tribulation. With Otrupon one must be very intelligent not to lose while trying to be slicker than the rest. Hence, not to be overconfident in thinking you are getting over on others. As the same, beware of someone desiring to get over on you in some fashion and gain leverage or advantage over a situation. In this oracle, folks easily forgot the sacrifices that you make for those you love. Hence, folks forget the sacrifices one makes for others in general. Don't be the same lead by example be the better person, but always cover your butt.

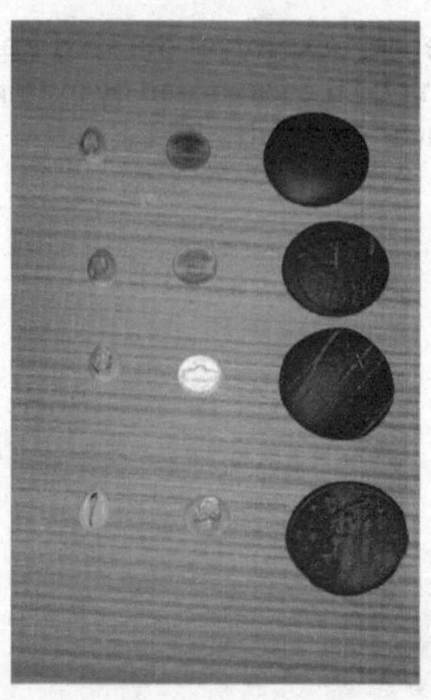

Okana Sodde - Simple Obi Toss - three down, one up; 3 tails 1 head

A straight "No," - don't, not this, something else and stop - check on something else desired at the time, or something is not correct at the time according to what you are asking... Many don't like to receive a "No" when asking or performing ritual work, yet how can divinities tell you what to change or switch with a "Yes." So, the "No" is a good indicator of the divinities communicating with you and specifying how they want things done. It's not always that "No" means not to do something, it can also mean stop change the order of things or find the best path. "No" can also mean it is not the proper time for obtaining desires, energies in your surroundings are not positively aligned, or conducive to favoring your actions at this moment. Also, there may be other rituals or much more work needed to be done for a positive outcome. With tossing an Itawa before followed by an Okana, it's obvious that it means "Maybe + No" ask for something else, in another way, or something is missing, there's a need to add more things – things are unsure.

Okana Sodde's are in IFa (**Okana**, Obara, Ika, Otrupon; Cowrie **01**, 06, 12, 14; I Ching (**Failure**, Authority, Peace, & Violation)

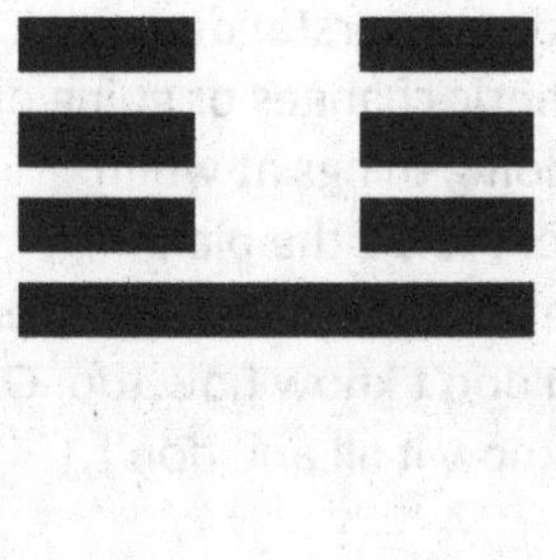

0
0
0
1

I Ching tetragram 15 - Failure; Yoruba Cowrie 01 - Okana; Yoruba IFa Okana

Okana is to be roped, bound, or tied. Speaks of letting go of things that keep an individually bounded. Also, means needing to bind or secure something so as not to lose it. It all depends on the situation and where the communication is leading too. Never do things without the consent of the divinities. Okana specifically speaks of all types of addictions; sexual, substance, chemical, or shopping i.e., all things destructive to individuals. Oracle of good habits that need to be acquired and bad habits that need to be let go. Okana is an oracle of drought; in essence, if you over-consume or indulge, you'll be left without. Speaks of only remembering God and divinities in times of necessities, or to suit their purpose. Then, when not obtaining what they want, don't believe that spirituality exists or works. Speaks of being dumb, not wanting to learn, or being stubborn. This oracle prescribes becoming educated for the sheer sake of becoming a more intellectual person or remain dumb for the rest of your life. People that can't think for themselves will have to rely on the intelligence of others and for this, they will have to pay. People that forsake education will have to rely on being lucky and God always compensates those with luck that need it for the lack of wisdom in obtaining things through means that don't require intelligence. But this attitude can lead a person down a path of criminology i.e., anti-social behavior, or dependence on others. Oracle of trickery, fooling, and double standards. The danger in this sign is to have a get-over mentality and not care about who they hurt to obtain their means. Speaks of being mindful, the need for being more understanding, and opened minded. Okana is an oracle of atmospheric changes or going out in bad weather. It is one of wrong timing and doing things at whim without proper planning. Always count on others to do the planning, scheduling, or troubleshooting when unable to do it for yourself. Never say you can do or try to do what you know you don't know how too. On the flip side, people that want to act like they know it all and don't, need to be left dumb.

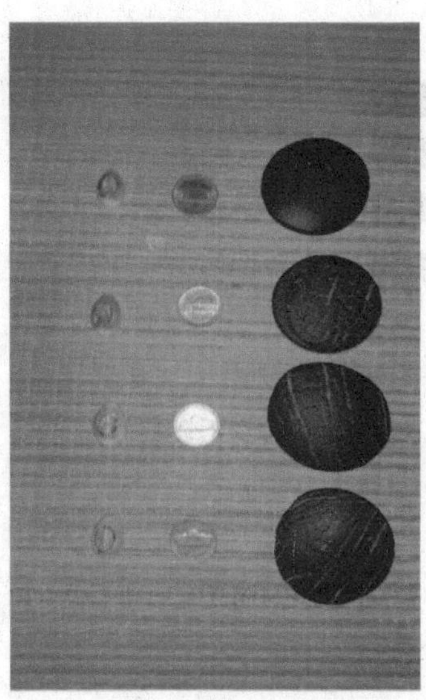

Okana Yekun - Simple Obi toss; all four down; 4 tails

"No" with consequences, danger, obstacles, or controversy. There are times where a divinity will give you Okana Yekun as a form of getting your attention for you to focus on other pressing matters. In this case continue asking on the various topics prevalent to you, until you hit upon the topic. Then, once the issue is resolve, divert back to your original questioning. Please, note that bargaining with a divinity can't exist. Many people do try, not understanding that logic dictates "No" is negative, not, don't, and should not. All questions must be one statement at a time, no double statements or you will obtain a confused answer. Accept only straight yes or no answers and reach a logical conclusion using this method. Noes are because conditions have not been met, actions follow reactions that position the situation to be off path. Always try to think of why you are obtaining a No to begin with. When getting stuck get advice from an elder.

Okana Yekun are - in Ifa Oyekun 0000; Cowrie Eyioko (02); I Ching Materialism

0
0
0
0

I Ching tetragram 16 - Materialism; Yoruba Cowrie 02 - Eyioko; Yoruba IFa Oyekun

As an oracle, it signifies the land of the dead mother earth. Where everything dies, decomposes, becomes nourishment for life to regenerate all over again. Earth is life-giving, then takes it back, turns it into sustenance, then gives it back again. It's an oracle of materialism, abundance, being greedy, and change. It's to take care of yourself, choices, and decisions made, so that blessings don't fall short, or be lost. It's an oracle of being indebted to the divinities. Promises must be kept there are unfinished or undone spiritual labors/tasks that need to be completed before other changes can transpire. It's an oracle of knowing how to be obedient, listen, and take advice, or suffer consequences because of not adhering to good advice. It means to take your time and do things right. Oyekun is to never think you know more than the forces. It is one of adhering to the rules and hierarchy of divinities, spiritual, and physical (natural) worlds. In essence, there is an order or a bigger picture than just you. Know your position, your role, and perform your duties as expected. It's an oracle of support and expansion of the family. Know that your actions can benefit, as well as, hurt others especially your family. Oyekun is to live long if you take good care of yourself, as it is to live short if you don't. Try not to do things alone, and don't be cheap especially with divinities. The more you give them, the more you'll receive from them. All that the Earth gives can be utilized for profit, and all that the Earth takes back is because it is owed to her.

Oracle of all debts needing to be paid, and when one does not pay one's debt honorably, dishonorable things will occur.

Part 3
I Ching Guide

How to toss coins, and expand your I Ching reading with Geomancy codes

As per traditional I Ching coin toss:

Heads = 3, Tails = 2; 3 coins are tossed at the same time on your divination mat, to obtain a numeric value of 06, 07, 08, or 09.

Obtaining a 06, or 08 means jotting a Yin-Yao   ━ ━   ;

as with a 07 or 09 we jot down a Yang-Yao   ━━━ . The three coins are tossed six times to obtain six lines or Yaos to generate a Hexagram. The Hexagram is noted by looking up the six lines on a Trigram table, matching the three top lines of your toss with one of the eight trigrams of the top row of the table; with the three bottom lines of your toss with one of the eight trigrams of the side bar of the table. Trigrams table:

Upper trigram → Lower trigram ↓								
	1	34	5	26	11	9	14	43
	25	51	3	27	24	42	21	17
	6	40	29	4	7	59	64	47
	33	62	39	52	15	53	56	31
	12	16	8	23	2	20	35	45
	44	32	48	18	46	57	50	28
	13	55	63	22	36	37	30	49
	10	54	60	41	19	61	38	58

Here is a list of the Sixty-four Hexagram names upon Hexagram lookup:

01	-	Heaven, The Creative, Force
02	-	Earth, The Devoted, Receptive, Flow, Give way
03	-	Difficulty in the Beginning, Break Through, Sprouting, Support, Hoarding
04	-	Youthful Folly, Discovering, Immaturity, Enveloping
05	-	Waiting, Arriving, Attending, Moistening
06	-	Conflict, Quarrels, Lawsuit
07	-	Army, Leading, Troops
08	-	Holding Together, Alliances, Grouping
09	-	The Taming Power of the Small, Small quantities, Little Bits at a time
10	-	Treading, Continuing, Conduct
11	-	Peace, Greatness, Pervading
12	-	Stagnation, Standstill, Hold Still
13	-	Fellowship with men, Getting along with people 11(Networking)
14	-	Possession in Great Measure, great possessions
15	-	Modesty, Humble
16	-	Enthusiasm, Providing For, Excess
17	-	The Following, In what footsteps
18	-	Work on what has been spoiled, fixing, correcting
19	-	Approach, Nearing, Finding a Way
20	-	Contemplation, Viewing, Understanding, Noticing, Awareness
21	-	Biting Through, Chewing, Grinding
22	-	Grace, Luxuriance, Adornments
23	-	Splitting Apart, Flaying, Stripping, Separating
24	-	Return, Turning Point, Retrogressing
25	-	Innocence, Without Embroiling, Un-wakened
26	-	The Taming Power of the Great, Storing Energy

57   -   The Gentle Penetrating Wind, Communication,
               Transmissions
58   -   The Joyous Lake, Openness, Happiness
59   -   Dispersion, Dissolution, Dissipating
60   -   Limitations, Moderation
61   -   Inner Truth, Knowing
62   -   Preponderance of the Small, Exceeding Through
               Small Things
63   -   After Completion, Completed
64   -   Before Completion, Not Yet

Now, let's pick Hexagram (55) Abundance as an example with
lines 02 from the bottom being a six (06), and lines 04 from the
bottom being a nine (09).

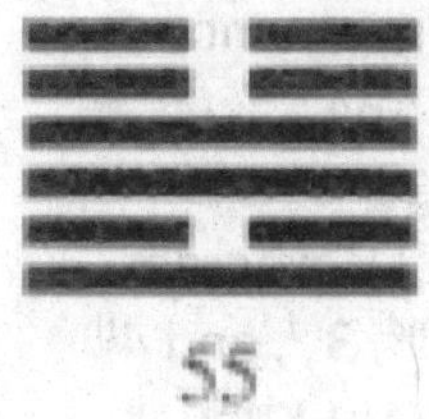

55

As per normal I Ching tradition this first toss is known as the Pen-
Kua. This is the karma or main topic of the reading. Notice that it
is made up of two trigrams, Chen on Top and Li at the bottom.

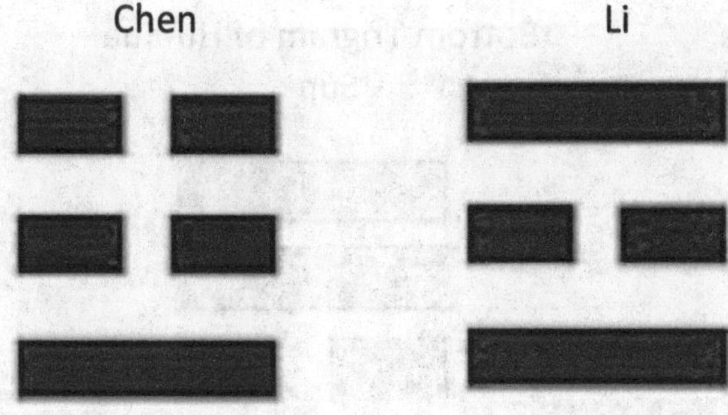

For further insights into the attributes of the bigrams and trigrams, look in the back of this book where there is an appendix with info on them. This Hexagram then yields three tetragrams that are cross referenced or matched to the geomancy codes. These three tetragrams are:

Bottom   Middle   Top

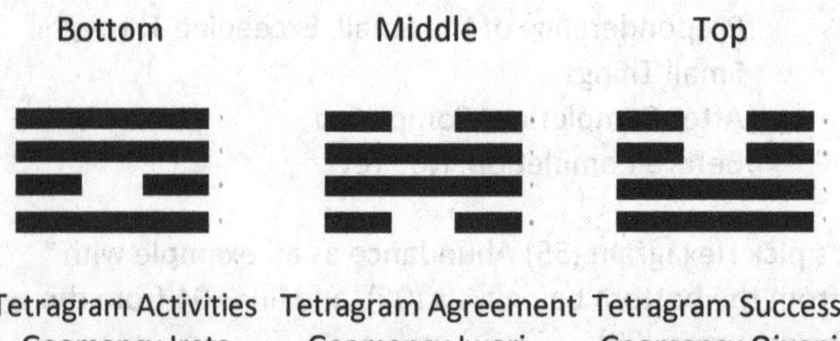

Tetragram Activities Tetragram Agreement Tetragram Success
Geomancy Irete   Geomancy Iwori   Geomancy Ojuani

For further explanation in the meanings of these geomancy codes look them up on pages 34-35, 53-55, and 62-64.

As per normal I Ching tradition, there is an internal Hexagram known as Hu-Kua. This is made up by taking the 2nd, 3rd, and 4th lines trigram, becoming the bottom trigram of the Hu-Kua; followed by taking the 3rd, 4th, and 5th lines trigram, becoming the top of the Hu-Kua. The Internal Hu-Kua gives insights as to the how or why? particulars of the karma being lived.

Top Trigram of Hu-Kua   Bottom Trigram of Hu-Kua
     Tui   Sun

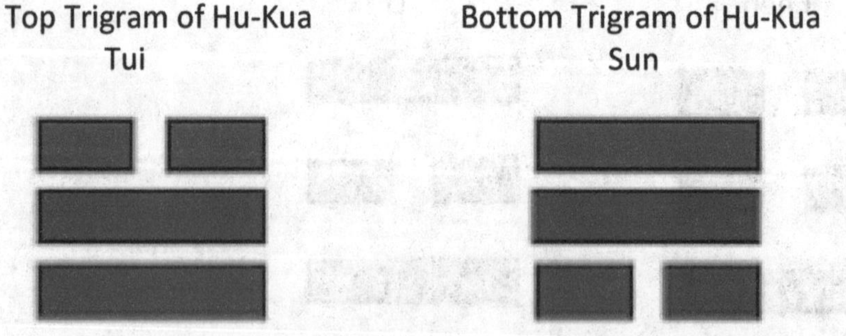

These give way to Hexagram (28) Preponderance of the Great

Note that this Hexagram will yield three more geomancy codes, and they are.

Top   Middle   Bottom

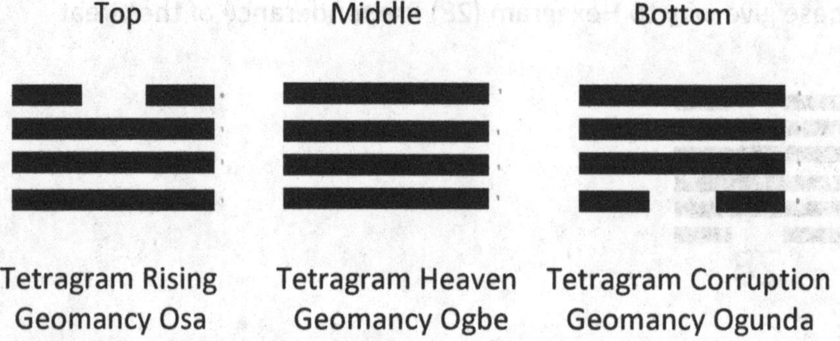

Tetragram Rising	Tetragram Heaven	Tetragram Corruption
Geomancy Osa	Geomancy Ogbe	Geomancy Ogunda

For further explanation in the meanings of these geomancy codes look them up on pages 50-52, 29-31, and 32-33.

Finally, here comes the third Hexagram Shih-Kua. It signifies outcome, or a possible insight on solution or problem solving to the reading. This is derived by taking any line 06, or 09 known as moving transformation line (Yao) and converting it to its opposite. A Yin-Yao becomes a Yang, and Yang-Yao's become Yin. Hence, we take 55 Abundance, and we change the 2nd and 4th lines. The 2nd becomes of Yang, and the 4th becomes a Yin. The third Hexagram becomes (11) Peace.

11

Our Lookup gives us - Chien (heaven) Trigram at the bottom with Kun (Earth) Trigram at the top. Consequently, there are three more Tetragram geomancy codes to add to the solution or outcome to this - I Ching reading.

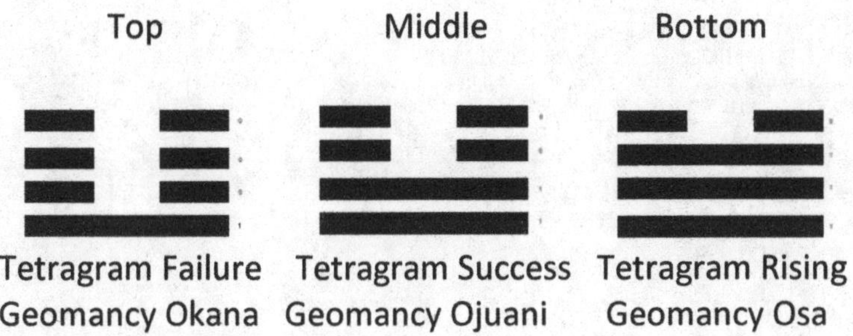

Top	Middle	Bottom
Tetragram Failure	Tetragram Success	Tetragram Rising
Geomancy Okana	Geomancy Ojuani	Geomancy Osa

For further explanation in the meanings of these geomancy codes look them up on pages 68-70, 62-64, and 50-52.

Interpretations Support

A word of advice - don't add more geomancy codes to the Hexagrams to read and interpret, than you are capable of understanding. For an inexperienced diviner this can be too much information especially when trying to apply it to your life situations. At first just start with one Hexagram extract the internal Hexagram and then the internal geomancy, this would be the bottom tetragram. Notice how in the book I'm not referring to the individual lines but have summarized the Hexagram as a whole. I did this so that one can concentrate on all three messages and keep things simple.

You can do the transformation of the lines and read the line advice from your other I Ching book. You can add more geomancy codes to the first, middle, and final Hexagrams (Pen-Kua, Hu-Kua, and Shih-Kua) as you become more proficient as a reader. Always keep your interpretations simple, clear, and concise.

Now that you have tossed the coins, obtained all three Hexagrams, and gathered all the tetragrams/geomancy codes that you desire to. You can read the advices, and begin to not just decipher the message, but also fine tune your interpretations for that moment. This is done through asking questions and obtaining a Yes, or No answers to them. Toss the coins twice to obtain two lines (Yao). These two lines together are known as bigrams. They are.

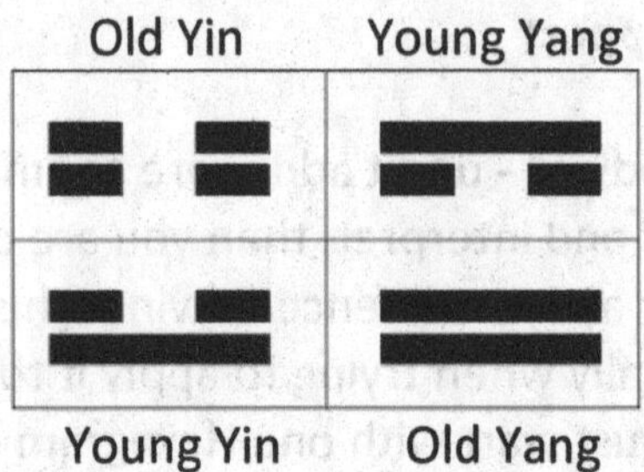

They make up two types of yes, and two types of no. The Yin's are no, and the Yang's are yes.
The difference in the Yin's is that Old Yin means no with consequences, Young Yin is a plainly no. The difference in the Yang's is that Old Yang is Yes with flying colors, and Young Yang means yes with further work needed (work in progress).

The Hexagrams and geomancy codes can be interpreted in many ways depending on what? An individual is going through at that moment. Asking yes's, and no's helps the diviner find the correct angle to the message.

In Conclusion, you have just made your I Ching reading into a very complex divination that will further enhance your prophecy as well as, advice. You can utilize any I Ching book with interpretation preferences along with the geomancy tetragrams in this book. Included in this book are the Sixty-four I Ching Hexagrams with unique author interpretations along with one imbedded tetragram corresponding to both Pen-Kua, and Hu-Kua Hexagrams. The Tetragrams explanations are the same sixteen geomancy codes found in the beginning of the book. This book is designed to function with both systems independently, and as explained above enhancing one another.

Sharing this knowledge and writing this book has been a labor of love. I've been supporting the spiritual needs of countless individuals for a very long time, and during this practice I've have encouraged folks to learn a divination system. A divination system serves as self-care, self-enlightenment, self-wisdom, and self-counsel methodology. When you can obtain answers from your spirituality, and proof of its truth. You are on the way towards making better choices and decisions, which lead to less mistakes and failures in life.

01 – The Creative (Heaven, Sky)

Heaven is creation and existence. Without the heavens/space, there wouldn't be a canvas for stars, solar systems, or other universes to have been formed. The creative is the embodiment of Tao (the way) forever moving and creating; the will of God (universal life force). It is now and forever ceaseless, tireless, and moving forward endless and generative. The creative heaven is an oracle of possibilities; beginning with knowing and acknowledging that we are and have been a possibility. Think of the probability of our existence, think of the supernatural occurrence of this solar system manifesting Earth. Let Earth be the divine proof of all things seen and unseen that can be made possible. In essence, if we are possible (life on earth humans etc.) that everything else that you might not believe in is possible. The creative emphasizes you being here and now forever moving forward adapting, failing, and correcting yourself. This can be extended to acknowledging our journey from life to death and back to life. This is the profound oracle of the I Ching that pronounces the existence of the universal life force which was not denied (Tao or will of God) and that's the way it is. For those that accept it wonderful, for those that do not, it is not in their time to do so. In essence, they are not there yet. Ask yourself? Are you there yet? Because this sign expresses that no matter how far you've come, and how far you think you are to go, there is always more. Hence, don't try so hard to tire yourself, but

allow yourself to get there, especially if it is right. This is an oracle were pushing forward and staying on the path leads to success. Hence, to persevere, perseverance takes you further. Oracle of creativity and the strength to move forward despite adversities. Although, it's always best to move in the direction of least resistance. Also, moving forward staying on path means, that the shortest distance between two points is to stay on a straight path. To know your direction and not deviate nor zigzag, because indecisions will slow you down and be a waste of time. This oracle prescribes being in harmony with heaven i.e., spirituality, religious inclinations, or practices. To act correctly and in moderation. To move carefully and be aware of dangers and surroundings. Honor, respect, and integrity are keen to succeed; be generous, kind, look to improve yourself, and influence others in positive ways. One must remain loyal and never betray those that support and serve you. To remain humble, let go of ego, pride, and prejudices. To know how to begin things and carry plans, ideas, and aspirations through to fruition. This oracle recommends not being arrogant; 1never boasting, bragging, or thinking yourself better than others. Not to harm or do evil to anyone. Never take advantage of others or those deemed weaker. But, to prove one's worth in being a symbol of hope, mutual respect of others, supporting those in their walks of life to find their purpose. But most of all, you find your purpose and reason for being. In this way, others and you can achieve happiness in knowing that your life has meant something.

Internal Tetragram Geomancy Code

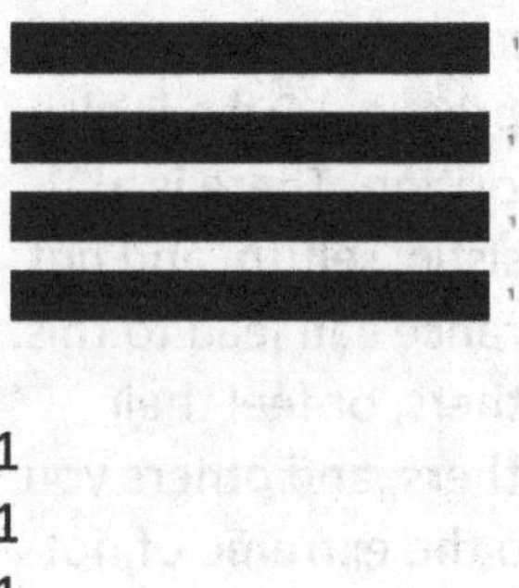

1
1
1
1

I Ching tetragram 01 - Voyage; Yoruba Cowrie 08 - Eyeunle;
Yoruba IFa Ogbe

Ogbe is the oracle of consciousness and will. So, you think so you are, where your mind takes you, so there will you be. From a positive point of view, it's where one becomes proud of one's achievements or how far one has come/traveled. It's to be on track with achieving goals and to see things through. On a negative thought, once you've felt that you've reached the top, then the worst that can happen is to suffer a fall or loss. This is an oracle of going through separations and adaptation to change; especially after making decisions that take you in the wrong direction. It advises not to lose your head i.e., give in to negative ego, or impulses. It recommends patience and protective actions. If your time is up where you are, then it's time to move on; life is not just one journey, but a long road that never ends. Speaking in this oracle are all situations dealing with the mind, thoughts, knowledge, understanding, wisdom, and ignorance. Not thinking properly will lead to confrontations, and one must beware of never overstepping boundaries. Support unity, but if needing to separate do so without violence. Know that all endings lead to new beginnings. Beware of actions that can turn into a justice situation, or lawsuit. But most of all to be organized or bringing order to your life. This is an oracle of being saved by taking a leap of faith and entering some form of spiritual practice. Ogbe is also, road, path, a11nd to be elevated to a new position. There is a tendency towards being or becoming narcissistic, selfish, and not empathic to others, i.e., arrogance and ignorance can lead to this. In essence, not to see through the eyes of others, or feel their concerns. It's not all about you, you affect others, and others you. Having bad behavior is imposing one's will to the extreme of not caring who they step on or who they injure along the way. It's there way or the highway; consequences to actions is sometimes overlooked when it comes to obtaining their means. One must be careful to bite more than one can chew. Things done by force will be met with contention and conflicts will follow. This is a mighty oracle announces blessings and successes that are to be achieved in ones' life. But, only through intelligence, wisdom, patience, and honorable means. All that can be supported by the will of God, and positive divinities in the right way.

HEXAGRAM

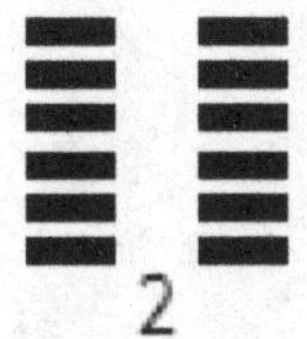

02 The Receptive Devoted - Earth

Earth is a place where life exists. Earth is a provider dedicated and devoted to the existence of life. Life regenerates because it has a place to cycle and recycle. This hexagram denotes having something to do, defining your purpose, or finding the reason for your existence. There isn't a day that Earth does not achieve its goal of sustaining a place for all that is materially or organically possible. Earth is our mother, and like a mother, it gives us life, provides protection, and nourishment. This hexagram teaches that we cannot be selfish because Earth is not. But Earth takes back, so it can continue giving. Hence, to be appreciative and give back to those that have given to you. We do not live just for ourselves, but for the goodness of others. In this way, we will always have in abundance to continue receiving and giving. Earth is receptive to the blessings that heaven has provided, and this is the opportunity for it to exist, if not for any other important reason. Too receptive is to be open-minded, respectful, conscientious, and empathetic. Earth materializes all things that are possible, makes things happen. It provides the construct for all that is negative and positive. Choose what you're to become, a producer of positive things or one of the negatives. We need both day and night, the dark and the light. Some plants, animals, and insects serve the day, and others serve the night. Some organisms exist in the cold, others in the tempered zone, and others in the hot regions. Are you as dry as a dessert or as wet rain? Such is the

way of Yin and Yang on Earth, where everything serves a purpose, and one thing is no more important than the other through the eyes of nature.

0
0
0
0

I Ching tetragram 16 - Materialism; Yoruba Cowrie 02 - Eyioko;
Yoruba IFa Oyekun

      As an oracle, it signifies the land of the dead mother earth. Where everything dies, decomposes, becomes nourishment for life to regenerate all over again.1 Earth is life-giving, then takes it back, turns it into sustenance, then gives it back again. It's an oracle of materialism, abundance, being greedy, and change. It's to take care of yourself, choices, and decisions made, so that blessings don't fall short, or be lost. It's an oracle of being indebted to the divinities. Promises must be kept there are unfinished or undone spiritual labors/tasks that need to be completed before other changes can transpire. It's an oracle of knowing how to be obedient, listen, and take advice, or suffer consequences because of not adhering to good advice. It means to take your time and do things right. Oyekun is to never think you know more than the forces. It is one of adhering to the rules and hierarchy of divinities, spiritual, and physical (natural) worlds. In essence, there is an order or a bigger picture than just you. Know your position, your role, and perform your duties as expected. It's an oracle of support and expansion of the family. Know that your

actions can benefit, as well as, hurt others especially your family. Oyekun is to live long if you take good care of yourself, as it is to live short if you don't. Try not to do things alone, and don't be cheap especially with divinities. The more you give them, the more you'll receive from them. All that the Earth gives can be utilized for profit, and all that the Earth takes back is because it is owed to her. Oracle of all debts needing to be paid, and when one does not pay one's debt honorably, dishonorable things will occur.

HEXAGRAM

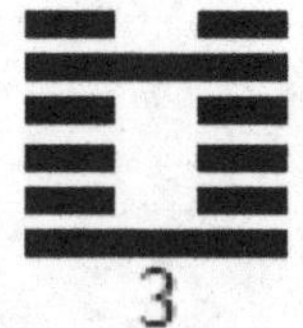

03 - Difficulty in the Beginning

Oracle of taking on new ventures. Difficulty in the beginning seeks to teach us that we should never do things or try to accomplish things through force. That we will be successful through proper preparedness. That we should plan before we execute, because when we don't, we will unavoidably meet contention. Difficulty in the beginning understands that to succeed in life we need to remove obstacles. We can remove obstacles through knowledge and understanding in what we need to do first, or what we need to have first. Do we need more education? Do we need more funds, do we need the support of others? What is to our favor, advantage, or what we don't have to our favor or not to our advantage? We cannot move forward blind because we will suffer expense and failure. Hence, to seek advice and counsel from elders and those that can teach you how to do things with less stress involved. This oracle stems from the idea of a seed sprouting roots, and a stem pushing its way up to the surface of dirt one moment at a time. The oracle embodies patience and perseverance without harm. This sign expresses the Yoruba understanding that we need to satisfy the necessary forces for the negative to give in for the positive to take hold.

23

23 Splitting Apart

This is an oracle of separations, breakups, and things falling apart. Negative situations have taken hold because of someone overlooked or did not notice what has been brewing underneath. This sign says that one should remain calm and allow for situations to take its course because it's too late to prevent it. The worst indication of this sign is to have thing taken away, removed, or a negative unexpected event transpire. If something has not happened yet, then there might still be time to prevent or sidestep. But this all depends on observing where and how one has been distracted, careless, or unnoticed of your environment.

0
0
0
1

I Ching tetragram 15 - Failure; Yoruba Cowrie 01 - Okana; Yoruba IFa Okana

Okana is to be roped, bound, or tied. Speaks of letting go of things that keep an individually bounded. Also, means needing to bind or secure something so as not to lose it. It all depends on the situation and where the communication is leading too. Never do things without the consent of the divinities. Okana specifically speaks of all types of addictions; sexual, substance, chemical, or shopping i.e., all things destructive to individuals. Oracle of good habits that need to be acquired and bad habits that need to be let go. Okana is an oracle of drought; in essence, if you over-consume or indulge, you'll be left without. Speaks of only remembering God and divinities in times of necessities, or to suit their purpose. Then, when not obtaining what they want, don't believe that spirituality exists or works. Speaks of being dumb, not wanting to learn, or being stubborn. This oracle prescribes becoming educated for the sheer sake of becoming a more intellectual person or remain dumb for the rest of your life. People that can't think for themselves will have to rely on the intelligence of others and for this, they will have to pay. People that forsake education

will have to rely on being lucky and God always compensates those with luck that need it for the lack of wisdom in obtaining things through means that don't require intelligence. But this attitude can lead a person down a path of criminology i.e., anti-social behavior, or dependence on others. Oracle of trickery, fooling, and double standards. The danger in this sign is to have a get-over mentality and not care about who they hurt to obtain their means. Speaks of being mindful, the need for being more understanding, and opened minded. Okana is an oracle of atmospheric changes or going out in bad weather. It is one of wrong timing and doing things at whim without proper planning. Always count on others to do the planning, scheduling, or troubleshooting when unable to do it for yourself. Never say you can do or try to do what you know you don't know how too. On the flip side, people that want to act like they know it all and don't, need to be left dumb.

HEXAGRAM

04 - Youthful Folly

What blind or inexperienced person can show me the way. Youthful folly is a sign of understanding we are inexperienced, immature in life, or lack knowledge. That we have yet to gain experience, and this does not happen overnight. Youthfulness is innocent when not arrogant, acting like a know it all, or allowing ego to get in the way. Through having patience being honorable, respectful, and humble, willing, and able mentors will come to enlighten. Youthful folly explains inexperience leads to mistakes, waisted time, and consequence due to immature actions. But through these lessons we are to learn and become experienced. Of course, when open minded enough to learn, and not stubborn, or in denial. We are students in this world, constantly learning new things. Allow for life to teach us through trials and error, successes, and failures. Then pass on your knowledge, wisdom, and experience to others. In this way, you will always be favored by the forces of mutual support and well-being.

Internal Hexagram

24

24 Return

Oracle of the return of positives after having undergone negative moments. The return of stability or things to begin turning around. This can signal of time of renewal that approaches or the beginning of moving forward after planning. In essence, failure or mistakes and living through should be at their end or nearing their end. But, because there is a return of positive karma, does not mean to stop being mindful of the mistakes that lead to setbacks or potential down fall. Be happy because of a sense of normalcy that's arriving. Yet, always remember that the struggle of getting somewhere is nothing compared to maintaining what you worked so hard to obtain.

0
0
1
0

I Ching tetragram 14 - Purity; Yoruba Cowrie 12 - Eyila; Yoruba IFa Otrupon

Otrupon is to be offended, to offend, or someone is on the offensive. Implying the need to protect yourself. This is an oracle of overcoming traumas; bullied, violated, disrespected, embarrassed, harassed, assaulted, cursed out, or abused. Speaks of wanting out of a relation, situation, job, and unable to find the way out. There is someone that wants to take over or win everything at all costs. They would do whatever it takes to get someone out of their way and obtain their means. Not to give in to selfishness, ego, or pride; also, to never be prejudice, misjudge, nor persecute anyone unjustly. Speaks of family betraying one another. Where mates in a separation battle over possessions and custody to the brinks of destroying one another. After a storm comes to calm as in - we need to weather storms; know how to outlive ordeals. Otrupon is an oracle of peace and harmony returning after having undergone situations of great turmoil and tribulation. With Otrupon one must be very intelligent not to lose while trying to be slicker than the rest. Hence, not to be overconfident in thinking you are getting over on others. As the

same, beware of someone desiring to get over on you in some
fashion and gain leverage or advantage over a situation. In this
oracle, folks easily forgot the sacrifices that you make for those
you love. Hence, folks forget the sacrifices one makes for others in
general. Don't be the same lead by example be the better person,
but always cover your butt.

HEXAGRAM

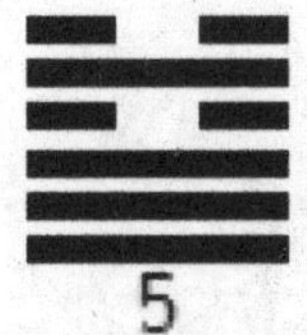

05 - Waiting

Waiting does not mean to nothing. This oracle announces success when an individual puts waiting to good use. To persevere is to push forward while waiting for the good or right opportunities to manifest or do things. During waiting we are engaged in spiritual meditative activities or spiritual healing rituals that will bring good luck to our forward movement. We have planned, and we are ready to execute, but the conditions must be favorable. Hence, waiting means to have strength to hold back just a little to analyze choices, decisions, or plan of actions before rushing forward. It is to exert self-control and not be overzealous. We must make sure that all preparations are in order, and we have organized things properly to move forward.

Internal Hexagram

38 Opposition

When opposition arrives, one needs to be diligent and advance slowly, not rush, nor push forward spontaneously. This is a time where someone, or something does not blend, mix, unite, and goes against others. Know that when people oppose one another problems will arise. Hence, meeting each other halfway in small matters can lead to better things or problem solving. Look at the benefits of resolving a little bit at a time and make changes that can bring about a positive outcome, even when there is opposition. Finger pointing, arguments, and stubbornness won't solve anything. Coming to terms due to mutual respect and using diplomacy will set things back on track and all will benefit.

0
1
1
1

I Ching tetragram 09 - Rising; Yoruba Cowrie 09 - Osa; Yoruba IFa Osa

      Osa is an oracle that signifies things being up in the air. Up for grabs, unsure, or insecure. Religious and spiritual work may support and solidify marriage, job, health, and family situations. But not all situations can be manipulated or resolved through ritual work, or spiritual practices. There is also common sense, logic, and facing reality. We can be our own worst enemy when being willful, selfish, and wanting things our way despite the greater good of things around us. In essence, never to give in, to selfishness. Obstacles occur due to not giving what is necessary to the divinities in time. All divinities and forces merit their fair share of attention. Spirit guides and ancestors need to be given light, especially those, which have died tragically or recently. Oracle of understanding the spiritual ideology of giving light, obtaining enlightenment, and finding one's spiritual purpose. Prescribes coming out of the dark and opening one's eyes to the truth. Some only believe their truth, never mind common sense, logic, and the obvious. Oracle of not living in denial, especially when things are staring you in the face. Beware of hiding behind pretenses as a

way of feeling empowered. Osa is also, an oracle of understanding investments, finances, and money matters. Never try to get over on others or earn a living through taking advantage of people. What goes around comes around. Not being cheap, yet conscientious, and sharing with others will always return benefits. This is an oracle of staying consistent in one's investments, businesses in the time will get better. Fast money doesn't last long, money earned throughout a period is much more profitable. not giving up. If money is not managed properly, you are sure to struggle. Osa is also an oracle of understanding female contribution in all things. It is one of understanding the feminine temperament and when the female energy is an asset. But also, beware of imbalances that cause this energy to become erratic. Osa is an oracle of getting along with others, and all people in general.

HEXAGRAM

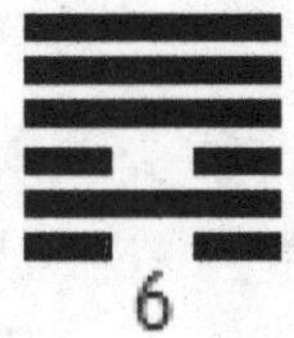

6

06 Conflict

Oracle of recognizing an unfavorable interaction or exchange due to not seeing eye to eye. Ask yourself are you this type of person (conflictive), or do you find yourself attracting this type of energy. When in conflict it is best to use restraint, so that things don't escalate. People are in conflict because one or many are unreasonable. Hence, to know what's the middle ground and parties take the middle as an opportunity to resolve any conflict. Conflict also needs to be recognized, if it's from within(internal) individualized, within a group, or external (influences) from outside forces. There are also times when we must admit that we need support in mediating the conflict and should seek help. Also, note that conflicts should have closure, so that future situations don't arise; reaching an agreement, or good accord brings success.

37

37 Family or Group

Blood is thicker than water, and everyone in a family carry mutual traits. Hence, in a family folks must strive towards getting along. Getting along with your family is like getting along with oneself. This is attributed to all members recognizing each other's roles and position; know yourself and what you can contribute to the whole. This begins with a good leader that can motivate and inspire others, as well as keep the family organized and intact. All members must maintain good character in meeting individual goals. The family or group is a collective. This means that all have separate responsibilities, but when putting them all together working in common interest, they accomplish optimum goals. Recognition must be given especially to those that have or share in the task of keeping everyone together. In relation to an actual family, one should ask if one believes in family, and if you do, will it require a marriage. Always remember that when forging a family, it becomes something greater than oneself. A family is a legacy, so nothing should be thought of in short term. Legacies are meant to exist long past our existence and withstand the test of generations.

1
0
1
0

I Ching tetragram 06 - Dissolution; Yoruba Cowrie 05 - Oche;
Yoruba IFa Oche

Oracle of the blood being thicker than water, blood being
the transporter of cells for living organisms to function. In
essence, blood is life. Oracle where money came into the world,
and today is the lifeblood of society, business, commerce, or
government economies. This is an oracle of fights over money,
and in some cases over livelihood (bringing food to your table).
Oracle of being cheated or feeling cheated. It's the oracle where
the money is cursed, or "the root to all evil." Human blood feeds
money i.e., the blood sweat, and tears of those that work to
survive. Rich folks curse it because many of them don't want to
lose it. Poor folks curse it because they don't have it, and it eludes
them. In Oche negativity stems from the decomposition of things,
corruption, failures, when situations fall apart. Uncleanliness,
impurities, or filthiness corrupts and generates diseases. Hence,
sanitize, wash, purify, and never allow germs, parasites, or viruses
to take hold. Taking care of one's digestion, and blood is
important to avoid illnesses or diseases from an early age. Oche is
an oracle of dysfunctional, disorganized family, relationships, or

affairs. The protection of the family, economic position, and not allowing for relationship problems getting in the way of happiness is key to being successful. In this oracle one is to make one's spirituality stronger through dedication, devotion, and being responsible with one's gift; otherwise, one loses the gift and gives way to the decomposition of all things. Oche is an oracle of protecting that which you've worked so hard to maintain. Love God and his divinities so you attend them, so will they support you in getting out of situations and resolving for better living. Oche is an oracle of needing to be saved through taking a leap of faith and entering a shamanistic priestly way of life.

HEXAGRAM

07 - The Army

What is the Army or an Army, organization, and leadership? Without a formation or structure an army is easily combated. Army teaches us that we need to count on superiors with intelligence and not try to take on tasks ourselves; knowing we need leadership and guidance. An army can only be successful as, is its strategy. And this comes from the minds of it is leaders. Individuals must ask themselves if they have what it takes to gather the right group of individuals, that are up to the task of leading. Is its leader worthy of respect, integrity, and honor and merit others to follow them? The oracle emphasizes not going to battle alone. An Army from a spiritual perspective, points to obtaining guidance from spirit guides, ancestors, or divine masters - that one is connected too. Learn to communicate with them, especially when unable to count on people.

Internal Hexagram

24 Return

Oracle of the return of positives after having undergone negative moments. The return of stability or things to begin turning around. This can signal of time of renewal that approaches or the beginning of moving forward after planning. In essence, failure or mistakes and living through should be at their end or nearing their end. But, because there is a return of positive karma, does not mean to stop being mindful of the mistakes that lead to setbacks or potential down fall. Be happy because of a sense of normalcy that's arriving. Yet, always remember that the struggle of getting somewhere is nothing compared to maintaining what you worked so hard to obtain.

01
0
1
0

I Ching tetragram 14 - Purity; Yoruba Cowrie 12 - Eyila; Yoruba IFa Otrupon

      Otrupon is to be offended, to offend, or someone is on the offensive. Implying the need to protect yourself. This is an oracle of overcoming traumas; bullied, violated, disrespected, embarrassed, harassed, assaulted, cursed out, or abused. Speaks of wanting out of a relation, situation, job, and unable to find the way out. There is someone that wants to take over or win everything at all costs. They would do whatever it takes to get someone out of their way and obtain their means. Not to give in to selfishness, ego, or pride; also, to never be prejudice, misjudge, nor persecute anyone unjustly. Speaks of family betraying one another. Where mates in a separation battle over possessions and custody to the brinks of destroying one another. After a storm comes to calm as in - we need to weather storms; know how to outlive ordeals. Otrupon is an oracle of peace and harmony returning after having undergone situations of great turmoil and tribulation. With Otrupon one must be very intelligent not to lose while trying to be slicker than the rest. Hence, not to be overconfident in thinking you are getting over on others. As the

same, beware of someone desiring to get over on you in some fashion and gain leverage or advantage over a situation. In this oracle, folks easily forgot the sacrifices that you make for those you love. Hence, folks forget the sacrifices one makes for others in general. Don't be the same lead by example be the better person, but always cover your butt.

HEXAGRAM

08 Holding Together

Can you hold things together, keep it together, or keep those together that are necessary for things to be successful? This is an oracle of things not getting out of hand. Things cannot be disorganized or in disarray. If this is the case proper planning has suffered and upon execution (trying to get things done) situations will not hold. It is important to have vision, foresight, and stay ten steps ahead of situations for things to be held together. Where can you see that there is a loose link a weakness within or surroundings that merits attention. Holding together is to tighten up.

23

23 Splitting Apart

This is an oracle of separations, breakups, and things falling apart. Negative situations have taken hold because of someone overlooked or did not notice what has been brewing underneath. This sign says that one should remain calm and allow for situations to take its course because it's too late to prevent it. The worst indication of this sign is to have thing taken away, removed, or a negative unexpected event transpire. If something has not happened yet, then there might still be time to prevent or sidestep. But this all depends on observing where and how one has been distracted, careless, or unnoticed of your environment.

0
0
0
0

I Ching tetragram 16 - Materialism; Yoruba Cowrie 02 - Eyioko;
Yoruba IFa Oyekun

As an oracle, it signifies the land of the dead mother earth. Where everything dies, decomposes, becomes nourishment for life to regenerate all over again. Earth is life-giving, then takes it back, turns it into sustenance, then gives it back again. It's an oracle of materialism, abundance, being greedy, and change. It's to take care of yourself, choices, and decisions made, so that blessings don't fall short, or be lost. It's an oracle of being indebted to the divinities. Promises must be kept there are unfinished or undone spiritual labors/tasks that need to be completed before other changes can transpire. It's an oracle of knowing how to be obedient, listen, and take advice, or suffer consequences because of not adhering to good advice. It means to take your time and do things right. Oyekun is to never think you know more than the forces. It is one of adhering to the rules and hierarchy of divinities, spiritual, and physical (natural) worlds. In essence, there is an order or a bigger picture than just you. Know your position, your role, and perform your duties as expected. It's an oracle of support and expansion of the family. Know that your

actions can benefit, as well as, hurt others especially your family. Oyekun is to live long if you take good care of yourself, as it is to live short if you don't. Try not to do things alone, and don't be cheap especially with divinities. The more you give them, the more you'll receive from them. All that the Earth gives can be utilized for profit, and all that the Earth takes back is because it is owed to her. Oracle of all debts needing to be paid, and when one does not pay one's debt honorably, dishonorable things will occur.

HEXAGRAM

09 - The Taming Power of the Small

Too tame is to subdue and with the small it means through little bits at a time. This is an oracle of success in holding back and only working on small matters for now. When communicating we can only persuade or influence those around us in small ways. It teaches also to be content in being able to achieve many little things in times of obstructions. In essence, something instead of nothing. Find and pinpoint the right places to exhort influence, then execute with precision timing is key to this success. We will find great achievements in not being greedy or forceful, instead be patient and pleasant.

Internal Hexagram

38 Opposition

When opposition arrives, one needs to be diligent and advance slowly, not rush, nor push forward spontaneously. This is a time where someone, or something does not blend, mix, unite, and goes against others. Know that when people oppose one another problems will arise. Hence, meeting each other halfway in small matters can lead to better things or problem solving. Look at the benefits of resolving a little bit at a time and make changes that can bring about a positive outcome, even when there is opposition. Finger pointing, arguments, and stubbornness won't solve anything. Coming to terms due to mutual respect and using diplomacy will set things back on track and all will benefit.

0
1
1
1

I Ching tetragram 09 - Rising; Yoruba Cowrie 09 - Osa; Yoruba IFa Osa

Osa is an oracle that signifies things being up in the air. Up for grabs, unsure, or insecure. Religious and spiritual work may support and solidify marriage, job, health, and family situations. But not all situations can be manipulated or resolved through ritual work, or spiritual practices. There is also common sense, logic, and facing reality. We can be our own worst enemy when being willful, selfish, and wanting things our way despite the greater good of things around us. In essence, never to give in, to selfishness. Obstacles occur due to not giving what is necessary to the divinities in time. All divinities and forces merit their fair share of attention. Spirit guides and ancestors need to be given light, especially those, which have died tragically or recently. Oracle of understanding the spiritual ideology of giving light, obtaining enlightenment, and finding one's spiritual purpose. Prescribes coming out of the dark and opening one's eyes to the truth. Some only believe their truth, never mind common sense, logic, and the obvious. Oracle of not living in denial, especially when things are staring you in the face. Beware of hiding behind pretenses as a

way of feeling empowered. Osa is also, an oracle of understanding investments, finances, and money matters. Never try to get over on others or earn a living through taking advantage of people. What goes around comes around. Not being cheap, yet conscientious, and sharing with others will always return benefits. This is an oracle of staying consistent in one's investments, businesses in the time will get better. Fast money doesn't last long, money earned throughout a period is much more profitable. not giving up. If money is not managed properly, you are sure to struggle. Osa is also an oracle of understanding female contribution in all things. It is one of understanding the feminine temperament and when the female energy is an asset. But also, beware of imbalances that cause this energy to become erratic. Osa is an oracle of getting along with others, and all people in general.

HEXAGRAM

10 - Treading

This is an oracle of knowing how to be. This means to know when to be sophisticated, or when to be casual. In essence, to know how to work with those that are simple as well as, those that are more complexed; those that are dangerous verses those that one is safe with. To tread is to be careful, hence how one conducts themselves is important. This is an oracle of exerting good conduct, because through good behavior we avoid problems. Regarding spirituality one needs to always maintain good conduct for development to heed good end results. What good is the practice of spirituality, if one has bad manners, indifference, and not know how to act in good character.

37

37 Family or Group

Blood is thicker than water, and everyone in a family carry mutual traits. Hence, in a family folks must strive towards getting along. Getting along with your family is like getting along with oneself. This is attributed to all members recognizing each other's roles and position; know yourself and what you can contribute to the whole. This begins with a good leader that can motivate and inspire others, as well as keep the family organized and intact. All members must maintain good character in meeting individual goals. The family or group is a collective. This means that all have separate responsibilities, but when putting them all together working in common interest, they accomplish optimum goals. Recognition must be given especially to those that have or share in the task of keeping everyone together. In relation to an actual family, one should ask if one believes in family, and if you do, will it require a marriage. Always remember that when forging a family, it becomes something greater than oneself. A family is a legacy, so nothing should be thought of in short term. Legacies are meant to exist long past our existence and withstand the test of generations.

1
0
1
1

I Ching tetragram 05 - Grace; Yoruba Cowrie 16 - Meridilogun;
Yoruba IFa Otura

Otura speaks of living in an inhospitable place. It's to be surrounded or live among con artists, and thieves. Also, to avoid being conned or tricked, someone is to be outwitted. Never be the first to know or know the most and the last to take advantage of opportunities. This is a sign of not being given recognition for your efforts or taken for granted. Don't take things for granted, life, family, relationship, jobs, or career, etc. Oracle of being too slow to take advantage of an opportunity due to being distracted. The person needs to have a sharp mind and keep things in order. Not saying you are going to do but doing it, especially with honor. The sooner an individual acquires the necessary skills, and identifies their talents or career, the sooner they will be successful. Oracle prescribes not allowing situations to drag. Bringing closure to situations will allow for one to go on to the next thing without skipping a beat. This sign doesn't permit delaying because carelessness and making mistakes will take hold. Oracle of knowing how to live within your means, respect, and 1worships the forces of God. How well and proficient individual

works with the divine forces, so will their grace bring them blessings. Speaks of dark forces robbing the person's luck, happiness, and economic well-being when not appeased or expunged in time. Yet, Otura is an oracle of resolving with good luck when situations are taken care of in time. Identify grace, gift, or being gracious in doing things with good taste, will win the hearts of others. And, with this comes the necessary support, not being alone, or left alone with all the weight upon your shoulders.

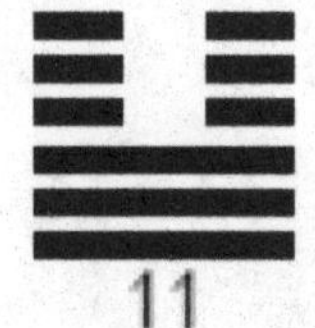

11

11 - Peace

A time of peace is a time when we can see, feel, and know that we have accomplished something or met something with success. This oracle means to work in peace, do things peacefully, and/or enjoy peacefulness. It's the break individuals need for a Day, Week or Month before going on to the next project or task. Oracle where Heaven and Earth unite in balance and unison, to be at peace in knowing that one is going to succeed, and all things will resolve. The oracle advises to remain focused and to stay on path with clarity of thought and purpose. Now, we can have peace.

54

54 Marrying Maiden

Wishing to marry, or for a binding relationship, as long as we both shall live, till death do we part. This requires aside from love and respect; communication with comprehension, patience with tolerance, and final asking each other if you still want to make this work. Granted ego, selfishness, pride, and insincerity must be tossed out the window. Marriage is about being all for one and one for all with the mutual goal of forging a legacy. If you are too young or too immature you are not ready and you will fail. If you are marrying for convenience, settling, or premeditated intent you'll pay in the long run, and it will fail too. Let's say the marriage is business oriented such is a partnership. But, even for this to be successful, not only should this partnership be for the same reason, but both must put in the work equally and balanced. One needs to offset the other, work as a team. In essence, recognize each other's strength and weaknesses, and both diligently work at improving them with each other supporting the other. Never forget to seek advice and counsel from those equipped with the knowledge to mediate conflicts all for the sake of the marriage remaining true.

0
1
1
1

I Ching tetragram 09 - Rising; Yoruba Cowrie 09 - Osa; Yoruba IFa Osa

     Osa is an oracle that signifies things being up in the air. Up for grabs, unsure, or insecure. Religious and spiritual work may support and solidify marriage, job, health, and family situations. But not all situations can be manipulated or resolved through ritual work, or spiritual practices. There is also common sense, logic, and facing reality. We can be our own worst enemy when being willful, selfish, and wanting things our way despite the greater good of things around us. In essence, never to give in, to selfishness. Obstacles occur due to not giving what is necessary to the divinities in time. All divinities and forces merit their fair share of attention. Spirit guides and ancestors need to be given light, especially those, which have died tragically or recently. Oracle of understanding the spiritual ideology of giving light, obtaining enlightenment, and finding one's spiritual purpose. Prescribes coming out of the dark and opening one's eyes to the truth. Some only believe their truth, never mind common sense, logic, and the obvious. Oracle of not living in denial, especially when things are staring you in the face. Beware of hiding behind pretenses as a

way of feeling empowered. Osa is also, an oracle of understanding investments, finances, and money matters. Never try to get over on others or earn a living through taking advantage of people. What goes around comes around. Not being cheap, yet conscientious, and sharing with others will always return benefits. This is an oracle of staying consistent in one's investments, businesses in the time will get better. Fast money doesn't last long, money earned throughout a period is much more profitable. not giving up. If money is not managed properly, you are sure to struggle. Osa is also an oracle of understanding female contribution in all things. It is one of understanding the feminine temperament and when the female energy is an asset. But also, beware of imbalances that cause this energy to become erratic. Osa is an oracle of getting along with others, and all people in general.

HEXAGRAM

12 - Stagnation

In this oracle Heaven and Earth move away from each other leaving mankind to do its will. It is a time where inferior people take over and chaos is allowed to disrupt the peace. Stagnation is to feel immobilized by the negative forces or darkness around us that does seem to allow us to move forward. It's amazing how when some, or a couple of people act up, they then contaminate others, and they act out of character as well. It is a time of feeling dissatisfied with situations. But we can look within to our spirituality to support us in being optimistic. That, although we might be going through the worst of times, nothing last forever. Turn inward and strengthen your connection to the divine, because this strength will help you come out of whatever the problems are. It is also good currently to take a step back from the limelight. It's not that you are going into hiding, it's more of an out of sight pause to allow the negatives to remove itself without damaging further.

Internal Hexagram

53

53 Gradual Development

All things that develop in time brings success. This is contingent upon acting correcting and staying on path and true to the cause till the end. All things that start off to quickly can reach a certain level, and then decline. Measures must be taken along the way to avoid the decline. Consideration must be given to the possibilities of things that can go wrong. When is someone not sincere or clear in their objective and fool others into meeting their selfish needs? This sign is one that prophecies the establishment of a relations, good relationships, or finding the right relationship. The relationship is proven to be successful if it leads to a good pairing. Both individuals or parties have found they match in goals and aspirations. Then with the correct temperance, motivation, and patience dedication and discipline will bring success. Gradual development ultimately implies sacrifice, effort, and consistency – solutions are not overnight. Also, one must be mindful of how to fix things along the way, in the event of mistakes and things going wrong.

1
0
0
0

I Ching tetragram 08 - Authority; Yoruba Cowrie 06 - Obara;
Yoruba IFa Obara

Obara says, "There can't be changed without revolution - chaos or torment." An oracle of wisdom, intelligence, and learning how to better live or coexist with those in your environment. Business related relative to marketing and knowing how to deliver goods to markets. The market rises, and the markets fall. It's where wheels turn/move forward, but there are times when we need to turn back or go backwards. Obara is an oracle where being proud leads to starvation, being left alone, or being put to the side. Oracle of success or failure, where the tongue, verb, or speaking can save you or do you in. The tongue can be used for evil, as it can be used for good. Good when it's used to praise, pray for good things, and bless. Evil went it's used to offend, false witness, and lie. So, mind your tongue. Speaks of knowing how to stay standing up and not falling after having worked hard in obtaining a position or move up in life. Speaks of good business relations when fair. Speaks of difficulties in maintaining relationships (personal, social) due to being difficult to satisfy. In Obara one needs to maintain focus on education and utilizing

one's talents or gifts to become successful. One is not to allow matters of the heart, emotions, or promiscuity to get in the way of one's success. Concentration and focus on achievements will bring happiness and many positive things. Giving in to pettiness, childishness, egotism, and distractions will lead to failure. The individual from a young age must learn to discern lies, and not fall into anti-social behavior. This will inevitably lead to doom. This is an oracle of planning, setting goals, and knowing how to execute the plan. Oracle of conquering and escaping danger when knowing how not to be in the wrong place, and at the wrong time. This is an oracle of not being a liar, learning that there is no honor in lying.

HEXAGRAM

13

13 - Fellowship

To be in fellowship is to be in fraternity. The gathering of like minds, common beliefs working towards a positive result. Those in the group cannot have their own agenda because then the fellowship will suffer, and all expectations will not be met. There shouldn't be hidden or reserved intentions. The group needs to be transparent within themselves and open to all contributors, because who you least expect of the group can make a difference. The strength of the fellowship lies in each member recognizing their talents and aligning it to a purpose. In this way individual responsibilities and interest work together as a collective mindset. In unity there is strength.

44

44 - Coming to Meet, Coupling, Meeting

People meet to discuss, brainstorm, or deliver a message. This can be a friendly hang out, business meeting, seductive meetup/getting to know each other, sexual encounters, or dangerous hidden agenda. This sign focuses on knowing that there is or will be a meeting of some sort. That you are to be or keep in control relative to the kind of meeting this is and never allow for any situation to become negative or dangerous. To always be aware of person's behaviors, attitudes, and intentions. This recommends preparation for the meeting and thinking of all possible outcomes to the meeting, so there are no surprises. Know that people in meetings align themselves with others, and look to leverage i.e., to be at an advantage point. If it's a one to one, think of the possibility of what they are trying to accomplish and how? Beware of false illusions or talking a good game for the sake of persuasion. Always be mindful, or conscientious of who's influencing who.

1
1
0
1

I Ching tetragram 03 - Activities; Yoruba Cowrie 13 - Metanla; Yoruba IFa Irete

Irete is an oracle of being sought after looked for or found. Beware of investigations, or being probed, and getting caught. Irete represents escaping, an escape, climbing out of a hole/ditch, or getting out of a rut. When desperate or in despair there will be someone or a situation will arise that will give way to the needed support in overcoming the difficulty. Irete is an oracle of upward mobility as in stepping up a ladder or striving towards bettering oneself, rising above the rest, or rising to the occasion. It is one of undergoing physical challenges, beware of early disease or injuries to one's limbs via falling and fracturing. Also beware of accidents, not being mindful. When it comes to women this is a sign that relates to difficult pregnancies. In general, beware of love triangles and promiscuity, which can lead to STDs. Learning how to attend to spirit guides and ancestors is important because it's a sign that marks communications with them. Learn to be obedient and listen to ancestral advice. There will be a reunion or gathering soon. The person needs much love,1 romanticism, and finding the correct mate to ensure happiness. This is not

something that happens trying too hard. It's something the
happens being at the right place and right time. In Irete religious
activities are much more favorable to the person's energy than
social ones (partying).

HEXAGRAM

14

14 - Possession in Great Measures

This oracle reflects obtaining all around well-being and good luck. Oracle of resolving situations, yet remaining kind, modest, and controlled; never arrogant or excessive. This sign prescribes never misusing your power, always winning the hearts of others so they favor you and all tasks get accomplished. Possession in great measures represents clarity in vision with inner strength to resolve. Value the advice of those that mentor you, and those that can contribute. Maintaining good character and a positive attitude and all things will meet with success.

Internal Hexagram

43

43 Resoluteness Breakthrough

This is the moment of seeing things through, resolving, or catching a break. Speaks of overcoming negative people, situations, or those that wish to keep one down. This oracle teaches to never resolve using force, when possible, but to win through small progressive advancement that might not be noticed by the enemies or obstructionist. Being aware of dangers and resisting the temptation of meeting it heads on. It is never a sign of weakness to ask for support or seek allies. This oracle's advice to never exhaust yourself trying too hard to overcome something. Negatives have a tendency of weakening and they're lies the opportunity to advance. Patience is necessary for breakthrough because all it takes is the right moment.

Internal Tetragram Geomancy Code

1
1
1
1

I Ching tetragram 01 - Voyage; Yoruba Cowrie 08 - Eyeunle;
Yoruba IFa Ogbe

1

     Ogbe is the oracle of consciousness and will. So, you think
so you are, where your mind takes you, so there will you be. From
a positive point of view, it's where one becomes proud of one's
achievements or how far one has come/traveled. It's to be on
track with achieving goals and to see things through. On a
negative thought, once you've felt that you've reached the top,
then the worst that can happen is to suffer a fall or loss. This is an
oracle of going through separations and adaptation to change;
especially after making decisions that take you in the wrong
direction. It advises not to lose your head i.e., give in to negative
ego, or impulses. It recommends patience and protective actions.
If your time is up where you are, then it's time to move on; life is
not just one journey, but a long road that never ends. Speaking in
this oracle are all situations dealing with the mind, thoughts,
knowledge, understanding, wisdom, and ignorance. Not thinking
properly will lead to confrontations, and one must beware of
never overstepping boundaries. Support unity, but if needing to
separate do so without violence. Know that all endings lead to

new beginnings. Beware of actions that can turn into a justice situation, or lawsuit. But most of all to be organized or bringing order to your life. This is an oracle of being saved by taking a leap of faith and entering some form of spiritual practice. Ogbe is also, road, path, and to be elevated to a new position. There is a tendency towards being or becoming narcissistic, selfish, and not empathic to others, i.e., arrogance and ignorance can lead to this. In essence, not to see through the eyes of others, or feel their concerns. It's not all about you, you affect others, and others you. Having bad behavior is imposing one's will to the extreme of not caring who they step on or who they injure along the way. It's there way or the highway; consequences to actions is sometimes overlooked when it comes to obtaining their means. One must be careful to bite more than one can chew. Things done by force will be met with contention and conflicts will follow. This is a mighty oracle announces blessings and successes that are to be achieved in ones' life. But, only through intelligence, wisdom, patience, and honorable means. All that can be supported by the will of God, and positive divinities in the right way.

HEXAGRAM

15 - Modesty

Oracle of not being arrogant, boastful, or proud. This is what it means to be modest; to act modest, and one will gain many positive things. Those that are modest obtain help from where they least expect and when they least expect. Modesty speaks for itself and never claims credit for good deeds. There are no enemies, jealousy, or envy because no one is envious of modest persons. Modest individuals always seem to help others innocently and for this get praised. Honoring others before ourselves is a sign of selflessness, and this can inspire others to be the same; not selfish.

Internal Hexagram

40

40 Deliverance Release

Anytime one releases tension, stress, or is released from being enslaved/imprisoned is a good thing. This is to be delivered, may we be delivered from or out of all negative situations and intent. Have deliverance is to be liberated, untangled, and unbound. There are bindings that are unnecessary, unneeded, and difficult to get out of. Recognize when you are putting yourself into an unpleasant situation binding to something that doesn't provide a blessing. This is an oracle of having a good outcome relative to being set free. It points to having been or being disturbed bothered, or unwillingly attached, even by mistake. There is nothing better than freedom. Hence, if you need to let someone go do so, for everyone's happiness. Selfishness, and control for the sake of egotism and stubbornness will never bring success in the end. They're many things that we must let go or let be free.

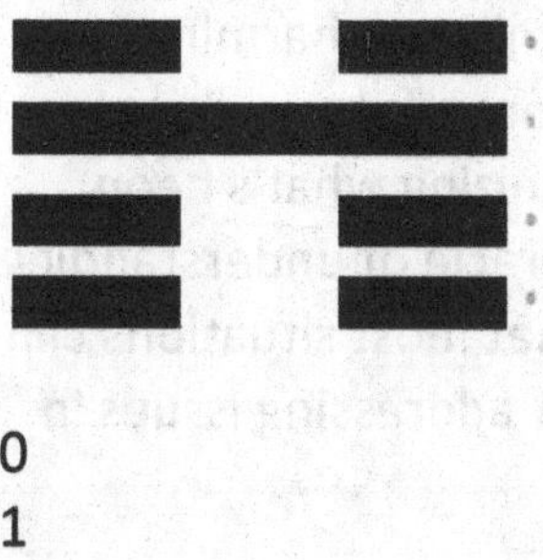

0
1
0
0

I Ching tetragram 12 - Violation; Yoruba Cowrie 14 - Merinla;
Yoruba IFa Ika

Ika means to know how to get around situations. It is an oracle of finding the correct approach to things. One needs to find themselves, and their correct way of being. But most importantly stability in life, i.e., where or what brings stability. If the individual has been kicked out, lost their job/home, their stability? They will need to help in getting back on track. Look to spirituality for this support or find those that can give guidance and ritual work to bring you back from the loss. Ika is an oracle of going to battle, or having to battle, along with the work that is needed to win. It's where we as young folks hit the road of life in a direction towards finding our profession, place, position, where one is going to be successful. If you find yourself struggling to much and going through obstacles and hard times. This is a definite indicator that you are not where you need to be. Ika is an oracle of avoiding battles or getting out them. Avoid spiritual battles with folks that utilize spirituality to do harm. Suggest too, allow elders or more experienced people to help you through guidance; don't try to be a know it all. Ika is an oracle of helping others and through

goodwill unto others, returning favors or someone least expected help you when most needed occurs. Hence, one is not to reject help due to pride. This is an oracle of the family not harming one another. Beware of being kicked out your home, job, work, relationship, or someplace due to not recognizing what's been going on. In essence you snooze you lose. Oracle of understanding what is evident or inevitable. Understand that most situations can be resolved just by getting out of the way or addressing issues in time.

HEXAGRAM

16

16 - Enthusiasm

A burst of excitement in the realization of something wonderful is always a joyful moment to experience. Enthusiasm begs precaution when it's blind to unknown events that have not yet transpired. In essence, getting excited when there is nothing to be excited about, at least not yet. This is what is meant by enthusiasm not becoming a waste of time or getting over excited over nothing. We need to be or feel enthusiastic about things that are tangible and real, not a fantasy or illusion. We need to jump for joy at the accomplish of a great ordeal, the realization of a goal, or aspiration that has final been accomplished or attained. Not what could of, should of, or would of...

39

39 Obstruction Hesitation

To be obstructed is to be blocked, held back, or not allowed to move forward. There are moments that this is due to the environment or timing. Time meaning year, month, day, season, or moment. There are positive seasons and negative ones. We can't always have things our way. Identify where the obstruction is coming from and formulate a plan for getting out of the way of what is blocking or understand that it can unblock itself. There are times in which we need the advice of someone wiser that can help us see how to remove the obstruction. Then, there are times where we need to hesitate or obstruct things for ourselves to avoid a foreseen danger. Hence, stop evaluate whether some situation was a bad choice, or mistake that is being caught on time. All deliberate hesitation or holding back will conclude with the correct decision as too when to move forward again. Hopefully, by then one has a better plan to execute.

1
0
0
0

I Ching tetragram 08 - Authority; Yoruba Cowrie 06 - Obara;
Yoruba IFa Obara

Obara says, "There can't be changed without revolution -
chaos or torment." An oracle of wisdom, intelligence, and learning
how to better live or coexist with those in your environment.
Business related relative to marketing and knowing how to deliver
goods to markets. The market rises, and the markets fall. It's
where wheels turn/move forward, but there are times when we
need to turn back or go backwards. Obara is an oracle where
being proud leads to starvation, being left alone, or being put to
the side. Oracle of success or failure, where the tongue, verb, or
speaking can save you or do you in. The tongue can be used for
evil, as it can be used for good. Good when it's used to praise,
pray for good things, and bless. Evil went it's used to offend, false
witness, and lie. So, mind your tongue. Speaks of knowing how to
stay standing up and not falling after having worked hard in
obtaining a position or move up in life. Speaks of good business
relations when fair. Speaks of difficulties in maintaining
relationships (personal, social) due to being difficult to satisfy. In
Obara one needs to maintain focus on education and utilizing

one's talents or gifts to become successful. One is not to allow matters of the heart, emotions, or promiscuity to get in the way of one's success. Concentration and focus on achievements will bring happiness and many positive things. Giving in to pettiness, childishness, egotism, and distractions will lead to failure. The individual from a young age must learn to discern lies, and not fall into anti-social behavior. This will inevitably lead to doom. This is an oracle of planning, setting goals, and knowing how to execute the plan. Oracle of conquering and escaping danger when knowing how not to be in the wrong place, and at the wrong time. This is an oracle of not being a liar, learning that there is no honor in lying.

HEXAGRAM

17

17 The Following

In what or who's footsteps are you following. Hopefully, this following leads to good things, because what blind man can show me the way as in the bling leading the blind. Watch who you follow, and what you follow. Who's the greater fool, the fool that's a fool or a fool that follows a fool. Following the truth, and all things transparent will never lead to false pretenses. Acknowledging that we have chosen something good to follow will enable us to have more successful movements that not. To be well rested is expressed by this oracle too because we cannot move forward being exhausted. Also, if you are to slow you might need to catch up.

53

53 Gradual Development

All things that develop in time brings success. This is contingent upon acting correcting and staying on path and true to the cause till the end. All things that start off to quickly can reach a certain level, and then decline. Measures must be taken along the way to avoid the decline. Consideration must be given to the possibilities of things that can go wrong. When is someone not sincere or clear in their objective and fool others into meeting their selfish needs? This sign is one that prophecies the establishment of a relations, good relationships, or finding the right relationship. The relationship is proven to be successful if it leads to a good pairing. Both individuals or parties have found they match in goals and aspirations. Then with the correct temperance, motivation, and patience dedication and discipline will bring success. Gradual development ultimately implies sacrifice, effort, and consistency – solutions are not overnight. Also, one must be mindful of how to fix things along the way, in the event of mistakes and things going wrong.

1
0
0
1

I Ching tetragram 07 - Obstacles; Yoruba Cowrie 07 - Odi; Yoruba IFa Odi

Odi is an oracle of great luck, and of having strong spirit guides, and ancestor links that when used properly and developed will bring about great things to a person's life. Oracle of individuals that can be a bit obnoxious overbearing or surrounded by obnoxious overbearing people and situations. The greatest downfall in the person's life according to this oracle is gossip, being nosy, and false witnessing. Also, speaking out of context, or giving out information to the wrong individuals at the wrong time. It's an oracle of having some sort of habit or addiction, i.e., an addictive personality. Substances abuse situations will lead to the destruction not only of the person's organism but of others and all happiness around them. Speaks of the creation of the marketplace learning sales, money management, having own business, or running someone's business. Oracle of feminism, and the gift of being a woman in bringing forth life into the world. The individual must be more objective, toughen their heart, and control emotions. Because this oracle is of being emotional, or emotional situations being hard for the person to handle. Keeping

a marriage will be a challenge and difficult due to emotional imbalances, jealousy issues, pride, ego, or constantly picking the wrong individual. Speaks of suffering childhood traumas that still affect the individual even throughout adulthood. Getting along with one's family can be difficult. Oracle where family members become enemies of one another. Ancestors demand family unity. Avoid indecisiveness, selfishness, and promiscuity. Oracle of a hole, crater, ditch, crevasse, or grave. Advice is to not make decisions or make lifestyle choices that lead to an early grave, for many pitfalls.

18 Work on what has spoiled

It is a time of correcting mistakes, fixing, or renewing things. There has been a deterioration or decline somewhere or in something because of lack of paying attention to it. In essence, something is broken and needs to be patched up or made better. Issues must be addressed, and there is a need for taking care of things or situations now. Procrastinating will not help things get too normal. You must find the right materials, employee the needed help, put in place a plan of execution and fix it.

54

54 Marrying Maiden

Wishing to marry, or for a binding relationship, as we both shall live, till death do we part. This requires aside from love and respect; communication with comprehension, patience with tolerance, and final asking each other if you still want to make this work. Granted ego, selfishness, pride, and insincerity must be tossed out the window. Marriage is about being all for one and one for all with the mutual goal of forging a legacy. If you are too young or too immature you are not ready and you will fail. If you are marrying for convenience, settling, or premeditated intent you'll pay in the long run, and it will fail too. Let's say the marriage is business oriented such is a partnership. But, even for this to be successful, not only should this partnership be for the same reason, but both must put in the work equally and balanced. One needs to offset the other, work as a team. In essence, recognize each other's strength and weaknesses, and both diligently work at improving them with each other supporting the other. Never forget to seek advice and counsel from those equipped with the knowledge to mediate conflicts all for the sake of the marriage remaining true.

0
1
1
0

I Ching tetragram 10 - Agreements; Yoruba Cowrie 15 - Marunla;
Yoruba IFa Iwori

Iwori is the oracle of your head's view on things or your
head getting around to the right thought processes. It is to know
what it means to think; think goodness as much as to know what
it is to think evil and be evil. Oracle of never thinking one is a
know it all, or to believe they know more than God, his divinities,
and the land of the dead. It's the oracle of scientific discovery,
technology, psychology, and all-around wisdom. Yet, maintaining
a level head being constructive and not destructive. Beware of a
mental breakdown due to overexerting one's brain in trying too
hard to accomplish desires. It is wisdom to know that what is
meant for you comes with little effort. Because it is meant be and
easy, it is right and the right timing too. What is not meant is
known because of the struggle that it takes trying to obtain it,
only to lose it because it was not meant to be. The individual must
beware of becoming overbearing, autocratic, or tyrannical
because one will end up alone. Where privileged individuals can
lose everything being overconfident, and making willful mistakes,
they need to listen to others too and respect their advice or

opinion. The greatest challenge is to learn how to obtain things by the grace of God, and divinities, not thinking all things come just because of your efforts. This demands great patience and allowing the divinities to bring things to you. Iwori's inner or external battle relates to finding their right place in the world. Frustration can come from the inability to uphold a position in society that is recognizable. They have a great need to feel that they are not just contributing to family, community, or society but also leaving a mark. Iwori is an oracle where families destroy one another through infighting, competing, and showing who's the dominate one. Yet, they as a unit become a force to be reckoned with when united or focus on the greater good of the whole family. Individuals should work on forging a legacy that lasts generations in this way they will truly make their mark on life.

HEXAGRAM

19

19 Approach

The correct angle to things. Approach is to align or find the proper order of execution to situations. The right course of action, or choices in tasks and agreements that lead to mutual benefit to all parties. Because the wrong approach will bring about failure and having to start over. Careful, intelligent approach with support of others leads to success. Negative attitudes or character will not contribute to the right approach on the contrary, it will delay and disenchant the undertaking.

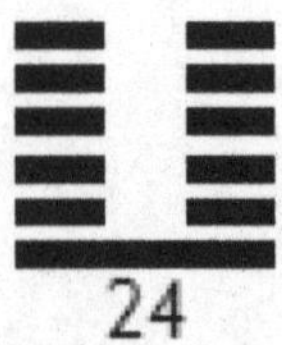

24

24 Return

Oracle of the return of positives after having undergone negative moments. The return of stability or things to begin turning around. This can signal of time of renewal that approaches or the beginning of moving forward after planning. In essence, failure or mistakes and living through should be at their end or nearing their end. But, because there is a return of positive karma, does not mean to stop being mindful of the mistakes that lead to setbacks or potential down fall. Be happy because of a sense of normalcy that's arriving. Yet, always remember that the struggle of getting somewhere is nothing compared to maintaining what you worked so hard to obtain.

0
0
1
1

I Ching tetragram 13 - Success; Yoruba Cowrie 11 - Ojuani; Yoruba IFa Ojuani

Ojuani means from riches to rags, and from rags to riches. It's an oracle of doubts, complexes, and potential insecurities. Persons have an overzealous ambition that when not held back can become destructive. Oracle where person's must keep their ego in check. Learn to live with others in peace strive for an education obtaining a career profession, or title. To be a responsible and not a careless individual, beware of desires; we can't have everything or everything we think is good for us might not be. Oracle of becoming easily bored with mates, so beware of promiscuity and STDs. People lose due to jealousy, and envy within a circle of friendships, work, and even family. Speaks of dark forces getting in the way of progress, external or internal. Oracle marks needing to be exorcised of dark energies/forces when prevalent i.e., noticed through not sleeping well, feeling haunted, or energy being sucked out of you. Beware of people that cling to you and become like a parasite, just as you should not be a parasite to anyone. Being sucked dry is noticed by how much you're losing due to relationship/business; not just money

but also one's peace of mind, tranquility, or space. In this oracle, one's family or mate's family can be your worst enemy or the biggest asset depending on how much they care about you or love you. Oracle of hurting or injuring the one we love through our actions or not noticing that one is doing this. Beware of being head-strung and willful as in my way or the highway. One must be flexible or understand when one has encountered inflexible individuals that don't contribute to positive things but get in the way and disrupt one's happiness. Beware of justice situations through being involved with people that are into illegal activities. Beware of becoming involved in illegal activities due to not acquiring a career in time. Oracle of never being envious of others, oracle of knowing who's on your side, and not damaging relationships.

HEXAGRAM

20 - Contemplation, View, Observation

Temples are for contemplation, sp11irituality, and mediation. Oracle of being dedicated to spiritual enlightenment and practice. Through observing that which is spiritual our sense perceptions activate, and we become aware of everything. Through spiritual practice, devotion, dedication and sharing of this knowledge. An individual becomes a beacon or symbol of inspiration to others. Teach others to observe and discover. Find the right environment to grow, contemplate on the wonders of life and spirituality. Don't be surprised if the peace and harmony you find, leads to you discovering yourself.

23

23 Splitting Apart

This is an oracle of separations, breakups, and things falling apart. Negative situations have taken hold because of someone overlooked or did not notice what has been brewing underneath. This sign says that one should remain calm and allow for situations to take its course because it's too late to prevent it. The worst indication of this sign is to have thing taken away, removed, or a negative unexpected event transpire. If something has not happened yet, then there might still be time to prevent or sidestep. But this all depends on observing where and how one has been distracted, careless, or unnoticed of your environment.

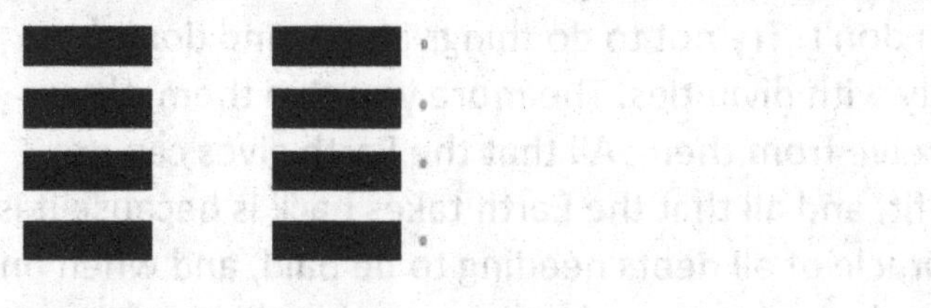

0
0
0
0

I Ching tetragram 16 - Materialism; Yoruba Cowrie 02 - Eyioko;
Yoruba IFa Oyekun

As an oracle, it signifies the land of the dead mother earth.
Where everything dies, decomposes, becomes nourishment for
life to regenerate all over again. Earth is life-giving, then takes it
back, turns it into sustenance, then gives it back again. It's an
oracle of materialism, abundance, being greedy, and change. It's
to take care of yourself, choices, and decisions made, so that
blessings don't fall short, or be lost. It's an oracle of being
indebted to the divinities. Promises must be kept there are
unfinished or undone spiritual labors/tasks that need to be
completed before other changes can transpire. It's an oracle of
knowing how to be obedient, listen, and take advice, or suffer
consequences because of not adhering to good advice. It means
to take your time and do things right. Oyekun is to never think you
know more than the forces. It is one of adhering to the rules and
hierarchy of divinities, spiritual, and physical (natural) worlds. In
essence, there is an order or a bigger picture than just you. Know
your position, your role, and perform your duties as expected. It's
an oracle of support and expansion of the family. Know that your

actions can benefit, as well as, hurt others especially your family. Oyekun is to live long if you take good care of yourself, as it is to live short if you don't. Try not to do things alone, and don't be cheap especially with divinities. The more you give them, the more you'll receive from them. All that the Earth gives can be utilized for profit, and all that the Earth takes back is because it is owed to her. Oracle of all debts needing to be paid, and when one does not pay one's debt honorably, dishonorable things will occur.

21

21 Biting-Through

Oracle of having the decency of excepting your faults, or blame. It is also an oracle of recognizing those that hurt others or injure as a form of intimidation. There are those that do things deliberately too or look for ways to disrupt for a desired affect or reaction. This is not a bad sign when used to enforce laws, rules, or ethical behavior. It's not wrong when we must bite through something (work hard) to eat it (except it); honor up, suck it up. But when actions are done with malice then it's not nice; hence, not be in denial of your actions. This is an oracle of potential justice situations, having explain or defend yourself, or paying for consequences of your action. Biting Through is also when we must bite our lips after causing something or having to take back after sticking our foot in it.

39

39 Obstruction Hesitation

To be obstructed is to be blocked, held back, or not allowed to move forward. There are moments that this is due to the environment or timing. Time meaning year, month, day, season, or moment. There are positive seasons and negative ones. We can't always have things our way. Identify where the obstruction is coming from and formulate a plan for getting out of the way of what is blocking or understand that it can unblock itself. There are times in which we need the advice of someone wiser that can help us see how to remove the obstruction. Then, there are times where we need to hesitate or obstruct things for ourselves to avoid a foreseen danger. Hence, stop evaluate whether some situation was a bad choice, or mistake that is being caught on time. All deliberate hesitation or holding back will conclude with the correct decision as too when to move forward again. Hopefully, by then one has a better plan to execute.

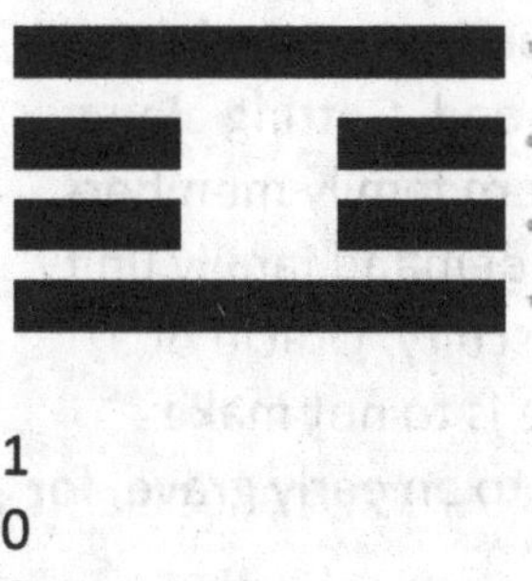

1
0
0
1

I Ching tetragram 07 - Obstacles; Yoruba Cowrie 07 - Odi; Yoruba IFa Odi

Odi is an oracle of great luck, and of having strong spirit guides, and ancestor links that when used properly and developed will bring about great things to a person's life. Oracle of individuals that can be a bit obnoxious overbearing or surrounded by obnoxious overbearing people and situations. The greatest downfall in the person's life according to this oracle is gossip, being nosy, and false witnessing. Also, speaking out of context, or giving out information to the wrong individuals at the wrong time. It's an oracle of having some sort of habit or addiction, i.e., an addictive personality. Substances abuse situations will lead to the destruction not only of the person's organism but of others and all happiness around them. Speaks of the creation of the marketplace learning sales, money management, having own business, or running someone's business. Oracle of feminism, and the gift of being a woman in bringing forth life into the world. The individual must be more objective, toughen their heart, and control emotions. Because this oracle is of being emotional, or emotional situations being hard for the person to handle. Keeping

a marriage will be a challenge and difficult due to emotional imbalances, jealousy issues, pride, ego, or constantly picking the wrong individual. Speaks of suffering childhood traumas that still affect the individual even throughout adulthood. Getting along with one's family can be difficult. Oracle where family members become enemies of one another. Ancestors demand family unity. Avoid indecisiveness, selfishness, and promiscuity. Oracle of a hole, crater, ditch, crevasse, or grave. Advice is to not make decisions or make lifestyle choices that lead to an early grave, for many pitfalls.

HEXAGRAM

22

22 Grace

Oracle of being graceful and doing things gracefully. To have grace regarding beauty causes attention and becomes desirable. When does something beautiful ceases to attract or be desired? When it's given the value of an ornament that after a while someone gets bored of it and replaces it. All things beautiful sooner or later tarnishes and deteriorates. To be in good grace sis to remain always full of graciousness that is timeless. Good character and good behavior without criticism or judgement is favorable grace. To work on your good graces is recognize your talent or natural skill sets and continually improve upon them. From a spiritual perspective may your grace never diminish, deteriorate, or tarnish. Hence, dedication and devotion to your spiritual grace will assure that you always remain blessed.

40

40 Deliverance Release

Anytime one releases tension, stress, or is released from being enslaved/imprisoned is a good thing. This is to be delivered, may we be delivered from or out of all negative situations and intent. Have deliverance is to be liberated, untangled, and unbound. There are bindings that are unnecessary, unneeded, and difficult to get out of. Recognize when you are putting yourself into an unpleasant situation binding to something that doesn't provide a blessing. This is an oracle of having a good outcome relative to being set free. It points to having been or being disturbed bothered, or unwillingly attached, even by mistake. There is nothing better than freedom. Hence, if you need to let someone go do so, for everyone's happiness. Selfishness, and control for the sake of egotism and stubbornness will never bring success in the end. They're many things that we must let go or let be free.

0
1
0
1

I Ching tetragram 11 - Limitations; Yoruba Cowrie 10 - Ofun;
Yoruba IFa Ofun

Ofun is an oracle of self-defense, where defending yourself is permitted. It's an oracle of great wisdom, growth, and grandeur. Yet, not to allow the grandeur to get one's head, or it will cause failures and setbacks. This oracle stresses seeking perfection and balance. In essence, greatness without humility or not knowing limitations will lead to demise and destruction. This oracle personifies living in harmony with society, nature, and your surroundings - Tao. It's where God's messengers/holy scriptures/words and testaments enter the world to teach mankind how to better live. Signifies losing one's life accidentally, or by mistake. Oracle recommends never overstepping one's position, being disobedient, taking unnecessary risk, or imposing will on others. This is an oracle of understanding boundaries, limitations, and knowing which lines are never too cross. What comes to mind with this oracle is "You're only as strong as the next person, which is equal to you or stronger." Ofun is an oracle of recognizing we can't know everything; we can't have everything, and we will lose thinking we are everything. Beware of

stepping out of line with one's actions or misjudging individuals. Oracle of being mindful of one's actions and the consequences that they can cause, as well as the actions of others along the same lines. With this oracle we learn to understand the nature of death. As in the cycle of a disease individual that slowly deteriorates leading to death. This cycle includes the individual and family coping with the process, beginning with denial, anger, anxiety, depression, acceptance, and finally grief. The spiritual process begins with death (reapers) coming to meet, hopefully in a controlled way, but as we know death can be sudden too. Then, the crossing over, extends to family acknowledging their ancestors, and initiating spiritual practices for the transcendence of their souls. Ofun represents processes involving the land of the dead, working with the dead, elevation or crossing over of the dead through ancestor worship.

23

23 Splitting Apart

This is an oracle of separations, breakups, and things falling apart. Negative situations have taken hold because of someone overlooked or did not notice what has been brewing underneath. This sign says that one should remain calm and allow for situations to take its course because it's too late to prevent it. The worst indication of this sign is to have thing taken away, removed, or a negative unexpected event transpire. If something has not happened yet, then there might still be time to prevent or sidestep. But this all depends on observing where and how one has been distracted, careless, or unnoticed of your environment.

02 The Receptive Devoted - Earth

Earth is a place where life exists. Earth is a provider dedicated and devoted to the existence of life. Life regenerates because it has a place to cycle and recycle. This hexagram denotes having something to do, defining your purpose, or finding the reason for your existence. There isn't a day that Earth does not achieve its goal of sustaining a place for all that is materially or organically possible. Earth is our mother, and like a mother, it gives us life, provides protection, and nourishment. This hexagram teaches that we cannot be selfish because Earth is not. But Earth takes back, so it can continue giving. Hence, to be appreciative and give back to those that have given to you. We do not live just for ourselves, but for the goodness of others. In this way, we will always have in abundance to continue receiving and giving. Earth is receptive to the blessings that heaven has provided, and this is the opportunity for it to exist, if not for any other important reason. Too receptive is to be open-minded, respectful, conscientious, and empathetic. Earth materializes all things that are possible, makes things happen. It provides the construct for all that is negative and positive. Choose what you're to become, a producer of positive things or one of the negatives. We need both day and night, the dark and the light. Some plants, animals, and insects serve the day, and others serve the night. Some organisms exist in the cold, others in the tempered zone, and others in the hot regions. Are you as dry as a dessert or as wet rain? Such is the

way of Yin and Yang on Earth, where everything serves a purpose, and one thing is no more important than the other through the eyes of nature.

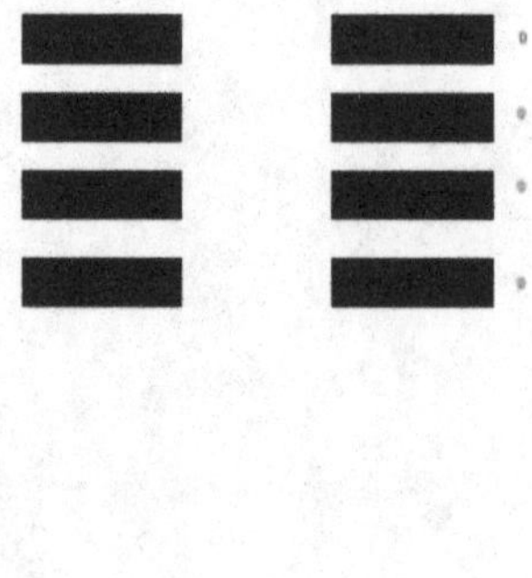

0
0
0
0

I Ching tetragram 16 - Materialism; Yoruba Cowrie 02 - Eyioko; Yoruba IFa Oyekun

     As an oracle, it signifies the land of the dead mother earth. Where everything dies, decomposes, becomes nourishment for life to regenerate all over again. Earth is life-giving, then takes it back, turns it into sustenance, then gives it back again. It's an oracle of materialism, abundance, being greedy, and change. It's to take care of yourself, choices, and decisions made, so that blessings don't fall short, or be lost. It's an oracle of being indebted to the divinities. Promises must be kept there are unfinished or undone spiritual labors/tasks that need to be completed before other changes can transpire. It's an oracle of knowing how to be obedient, listen, and take advice, or suffer consequences because of not adhering to good advice. It means to take your time and do things right. Oyekun is to never think you know more than the forces. It is one of adhering to the rules and hierarchy of divinities, spiritual, and physical (natural) worlds. In essence, there is an order or a bigger picture than just you. Know your position, your role, and perform your duties as expected. It's an oracle of support and expansion of the family. Know that your

actions can benefit, as well as, hurt others especially your family. Oyekun is to live long if you take good care of yourself, as it is to live short if you don't. Try not to do things alone, and don't be cheap especially with divinities. The more you give them, the more you'll receive from them. All that the Earth gives can be utilized for profit, and all that the Earth takes back is because it is owed to her. Oracle of all debts needing to be paid, and when one does not pay one's debt honorably, dishonorable things will occur.

24 Return

Oracle of the return of positives after having undergone negative moments. The return of stability or things to begin turning around. This can signal of time of renewal that approaches or the beginning of moving forward after planning. In essence, failure or mistakes and living through should be at their end or nearing their end. But, because there is a return of positive karma, does not mean to stop being mindful of the mistakes that lead to setbacks or potential down fall. Be happy because of a sense of normalcy that's arriving. Yet, always remember that the struggle of getting somewhere is nothing compared to maintaining what you worked so hard to obtain.

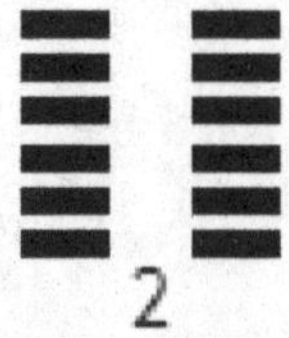

02 The Receptive Devoted - Earth

Earth is a place where life exists. Earth is a provider dedicated and devoted to the existence of life. Life regenerates because it has a place to cycle and recycle. This hexagram denotes having something to do, defining your purpose, or finding the reason for your existence. There isn't a day that Earth does not achieve its goal of sustaining a place for all that is materially or organically possible. Earth is our mother, and like a mother, it gives us life, provides protection, and nourishment. This hexagram teaches that we cannot be selfish because Earth is not. But Earth takes back, so it can continue giving. Hence, to be appreciative and give back to those that have given to you. We do not live just for ourselves, but for the goodness of others. In this way, we will always have in abundance to continue receiving and giving. Earth is receptive to the blessings that heaven has provided, and this is the opportunity for it to exist, if not for any other important reason. Too receptive is to be open-minded, respectful, conscientious, and empathetic. Earth materializes all things that are possible, makes things happen. It provides the construct for all that is negative and positive. Choose what you're to become, a producer of positive things or one of the negatives. We need both day and night, the dark and the light. Some plants, animals, and insects serve the day, and others serve the night. Some organisms exist in the cold, others in the tempered zone, and others in the hot regions. Are you as dry as a dessert or as wet rain? Such is the

way of Yin and Yang on Earth, where everything serves a purpose, and one thing is no more important than the other through the eyes of nature.

0
0
0
1

I Ching tetragram 15 - Failure; Yoruba Cowrie 01 - Okana; Yoruba IFa Okana

Okana is to be roped, bound, or tied. Speaks of letting go of things that keep an individually bounded. Also, means needing to bind or secure something so as not to lose it. It all depends on the situation and where the communication is leading too. Never do things without the consent of the divinities. Okana specifically speaks of all types of addictions; sexual, substance, chemical, or shopping i.e., all things destructive to individuals. Oracle of good habits that need to be acquired and bad habits that need to be let go. Okana is an oracle of drought; in essence, if you over-consume or indulge, you'll be left without. Speaks of only remembering God and divinities in times of necessities, or to suit their purpose. Then, when not obtaining what they want, don't believe that spirituality exists or works. Speaks of being dumb, not wanting to learn, or being stubborn. This oracle prescribes becoming educated for the sheer sake of becoming a more intellectual person or remain dumb for the rest of your life. People that can't think for themselves will have to rely on the intelligence of others and for this, they will have to pay. People that forsake education

will have to rely on being lucky and God always compensates those with luck that need it for the lack of wisdom in obtaining things through means that don't require intelligence. But this attitude can lead a person down a path of criminology i.e., anti-social behavior, or dependence on others. Oracle of trickery, fooling, and double standards. The danger in this sign is to have a get-over mentality and not care about who they hurt to obtain their means. Speaks of being mindful, the need for being more understanding, and opened minded. Okana is an oracle of atmospheric changes or going out in bad weather. It is one of wrong timing and doing things at whim without proper planning. Always count on others to do the planning, scheduling, or troubleshooting when unable to do it for yourself. Never say you can do or try to do what you know you don't know how too. On the flip side, people that want to act like they know it all and don't, need to be left dumb.

HEXAGRAM

25

25 - Innocence - The Unexpected

When we are innocent, we can make mistakes due to lack of experience, or overlooking things, due to ignorance. Many things can happen unexpectedly in our lives due to innocence or inexperience. There are positives to the unexpected and negatives, such as innocent mistakes or lying to save your skin that backfires. A positive that we can't be blamed for not knowing. To the innocent or inexperienced it is recommended that they always use caution when meeting people. Your innocence can que the savvy (slick or con) that you are prey and can be easily taken advantage of. Individuals must avoid being gullible, or vulnerable due to lack of knowledge. Another part of lacking knowledge is the dependence on others. For the innocent learning or becoming well educated sooner than later is a plus. Also, look within yourself when you are the experienced taking advantage of the more vulnerable, and know that it can come right back. Because we all take turns being innocent.

53

53 Gradual Development

All things that develop in time brings success. This is contingent upon acting correcting and staying on path and true to the cause till the end. All things that start off to quickly can reach a certain level, and then decline. Measures must be taken along the way to avoid the decline. Consideration must be given to the possibilities of things that can go wrong. When is someone not sincere or clear in their objective and fool others into meeting their selfish needs? This sign is one that prophecies the establishment of a relations, good relationships, or finding the right relationship. The relationship is proven to be successful if it leads to a good pairing. Both individuals or parties have found they match in goals and aspirations. Then with the correct temperance, motivation, and patience dedication and discipline will bring success. Gradual development ultimately implies sacrifice, effort, and consistency – solutions are not overnight. Also, one must be mindful of how to fix things along the way, in the event of mistakes and things going wrong.

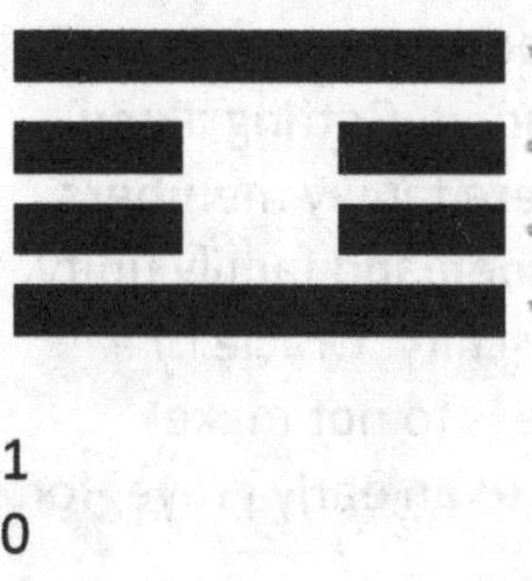

1
0
0
1

I Ching tetragram 07 - Obstacles; Yoruba Cowrie 07 - Odi; Yoruba IFa Odi

Odi is an oracle of great luck, and of having strong spirit guides, and ancestor links that when used properly and developed will bring about great things to a person's life. Oracle of individuals that can be a bit obnoxious overbearing or surrounded by obnoxious overbearing people and situations. The greatest downfall in the person's life according to this oracle is gossip, being nosy, and false witnessing. Also, speaking out of context, or giving out information to the wrong individuals at the wrong time. It's an oracle of having some sort of habit or addiction, i.e., an addictive personality. Substances abuse situations will lead to the destruction not only of the person's organism but of others and all happiness around them. Speaks of the creation of the marketplace learning sales, money management, having own business, or running someone's business. Oracle of feminism, and the gift of being a woman in bringing forth life into the world. The individual must be more objective, toughen their heart, and control emotions. Because this oracle is of being emotional, or emotional situations being hard for the person to handle. Keeping

a marriage will be a challenge and difficult due to emotional imbalances, jealousy issues, pride, ego, or constantly picking the wrong individual. Speaks of suffering childhood traumas that still affect the individual even throughout adulthood. Getting along with one's family can be difficult. Oracle where family members become enemies of one another. Ancestors demand family unity. Avoid indecisiveness, selfishness, and promiscuity. Oracle of a hole, crater, ditch, crevasse, or grave. Advice is to not make decisions or make lifestyle choices that lead to an early grave, for many pitfalls.

HEXAGRAM

26

The Taming Power of the Great - Storing Energy

     Oracle of self-control and will-power, the strength inside to subdue oneself. When need be one holds back for the right reasons. This oracle prescribes constancy and discipline where work is concerned in an effort towards meeting aspirations. When one has studied situations and devised a plan, one must maintain inner focus and follow the plan without deviations. Only then, can one experience the fruits of its labor. This oracle expresses setting rules, regulations, and standards for maintaining an order to things for their accomplishment. Following these directives without overzealous leaping into something else will lead to success.

Internal Hexagram

54

54 Marrying Maiden

Wishing to marry, or for a binding relationship as we both shall live, till death do we part. This requires aside from love and respect; communication with comprehension, patience with tolerance, and final asking each other if you still want to make this work. Granted ego, selfishness, pride, and insincerity must be tossed out the window. Marriage is about being all for one and one for all with the mutual goal of forging a legacy. If you are too young or too immature you are not ready and you will fail. If you are marrying for convenience, settling, or premeditated intent you'll pay in the long run, and it will fail too. Let's say the marriage is business oriented such is a partnership. But, even for this to be successful, not only should this partnership be for the same reason, but both must put in the work equally and balanced. One needs to offset the other, work as a team. In essence, recognize each other's strength and weaknesses, and both diligently work at improving them with each other supporting the other. Never forget to seek advice and counsel from those equipped with the knowledge to mediate conflicts all for the sake of the marriage remaining true.

0
1
1
1

I Ching tetragram 09 - Rising; Yoruba Cowrie 09 - Osa; Yoruba IFa Osa

      Osa is an oracle that signifies things being up in the air. Up for grabs, unsure, or insecure. Religious and spiritual work may support and solidify marriage, job, health, and family situations. But not all situations can be manipulated or resolved through ritual work, or spiritual practices. There is also common sense, logic, and facing reality. We can be our own worst enemy when being willful, selfish, and wanting things our way despite the greater good of things around us. In essence, never to give in, to selfishness. Obstacles occur due to not giving what is necessary to the divinities in time. All divinities and forces merit their fair share of attention. Spirit guides and ancestors need to be given light, especially those, which have died tragically or recently. Oracle of understanding the spiritual ideology of giving light, obtaining enlightenment, and finding one's spiritual purpose. Prescribes coming out of the dark and opening one's eyes to the truth. Some only believe their truth, never mind common sense, logic, and the obvious. Oracle of not living in denial, especially when things are staring you in the face. Beware of hiding behind pretenses as a

way of feeling empowered. Osa is also, an oracle of understanding investments, finances, and money matters. Never try to get over on others or earn a living through taking advantage of people. What goes around comes around. Not being cheap, yet conscientious, and sharing with others will always return benefits. This is an oracle of staying consistent in one's investments, businesses in the time will get better. Fast money doesn't last long, money earned throughout a period is much more profitable. not giving up. If money is not managed properly, you are sure to struggle. Osa is also an oracle of understanding female contribution in all things. It is one of understanding the feminine temperament and when the female energy is an asset. But also, beware of imbalances that cause this energy to become erratic. Osa is an oracle of getting along with others, and all people in general.

HEXAGRAM

27

27 The Corners of the Mouth

There are good reasons for opening one's mouth, and other reasons for keeping it shut.
This oracle says that we can tell a lot about individuals by what they nourish themselves with. There are those that nourish the belly, those that nourish the mind, those that nourish their bodies, those that nourish spirituality, and those only desire to nourish tongues with gossip and falsehoods. In essence, too much of anything is not good, as in we need a balance even when it comes to what we decide to nourish ourselves with. Food can enter the mouth tasting very good, yet leave the body smelling foul, as in it decays within the digestive system. When is something good for you and when is something just not right or no longer of good taste? We must look around and seek the truths, speak truths, and discern lies. When do certain people or situations cease to provide something that is of worth, useful, and tangible. Actions can cease to be of worth when they don't provide something of value, as in when they hurt others. This is an oracle of working on physical, emotional, psychological, and spiritual well-being, not stigmatization, discrimination, stereotyping, or giving in to hate and prejudices.

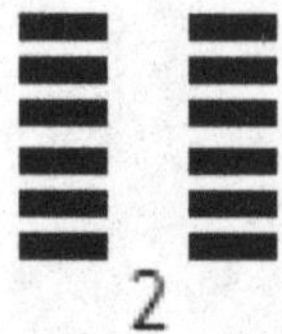

02 The Receptive Devoted - Earth

Earth is a place where life exists. Earth is a provider dedicated and devoted to the existence of life. Life regenerates because it has a place to cycle and recycle. This hexagram denotes having something to do, defining your purpose, or finding the reason for your existence. There isn't a day that Earth does not achieve its goal of sustaining a place for all that is materially or organically possible. Earth is our mother, and like a mother, it gives us life, provides protection, and nourishment. This hexagram teaches that we cannot be selfish because Earth is not. But Earth takes back, so it can continue giving. Hence, to be appreciative and give back to those that have given to you. We do not live just for ourselves, but for the goodness of others. In this way, we will always have in abundance to continue receiving and giving. Earth is receptive to the blessings that heaven has provided, and this is the opportunity for it to exist, if not for any other important reason. Too receptive is to be open-minded, respectful, conscientious, and empathetic. Earth materializes all things that are possible, makes things happen. It provides the construct for all that is negative and positive. Choose what you're to become, a producer of positive things or one of the negatives. We need both day and night, the dark and the light. Some plants, animals, and insects serve the day, and others serve the night. Some organisms exist in the cold, others in the tempered zone, and others in the hot regions. Are you as dry as a dessert or as wet rain? Such is the

way of Yin and Yang on Earth, where everything serves a purpose, and one thing is no more important than the other through the eyes of nature.

0
0
0
1

I Ching tetragram 15 - Failure; Yoruba Cowrie 01 - Okana; Yoruba IFa Okana

Okana is to be roped, bound, or tied. Speaks of letting go of things that keep an individually bounded. Also, means needing to bind or secure something so as not to lose it. It all depends on the situation and where the communication is leading too. Never do things without the consent of the divinities. Okana specifically speaks of all types of addictions; sexual, substance, chemical, or shopping i.e., all things destructive to individuals. Oracle of good habits that need to be acquired and bad habits that need to be let go. Okana is an oracle of drought; in essence, if you over-consume or indulge, you'll be left without. Speaks of only remembering God and divinities in times of necessities, or to suit their purpose. Then, when not obtaining what they want, don't believe that spirituality exists or works. Speaks of being dumb, not wanting to learn, or being stubborn. This oracle prescribes becoming educated for the sheer sake of becoming a more intellectual person or remain dumb for the rest of your life. People that can't think for themselves will have to rely on the intelligence of others and for this, they will have to pay. People that forsake education

will have to rely on being lucky and God always compensates those with luck that need it for the lack of wisdom in obtaining things through means that don't require intelligence. But this attitude can lead a person down a path of criminology i.e., anti-social behavior, or dependence on others. Oracle of trickery, fooling, and double standards. The danger in this sign is to have a get-over mentality and not care about who they hurt to obtain their means. Speaks of being mindful, the need for being more understanding, and opened minded. Okana is an oracle of atmospheric changes or going out in bad weather. It is one of wrong timing and doing things at whim without proper planning. Always count on others to do the planning, scheduling, or troubleshooting when unable to do it for yourself. Never say you can do or try to do what you know you don't know how too. On the flip side, people that want to act like they know it all and don't, need to be left dumb.

HEXAGRAM

28 - Preponderance of the Great - Excessiveness or Extra

Oracle of excessiveness, extra, too much to handle, or overindulging. This also means too beware of gluttony, greed, or exaggeration. The advice is to understand when something is too much, overkill, or know when something is being overdone. Something will break when it is in excess, it stresses that all things must be handled correctly and with care for what things to not break. Proper due diligence (homework), evaluations, and executions will give way to successful outcome. Excess, or extra is good when it meets expectations or surpasses them. Preponderance of the great also means to accept change or know that change is unavoidable no matter how much we try to push forward or hold back. The individual might want to but forces more powerful are pushing for things to manifest despite attempting to control them.

01 - The Creative (Heaven, Sky)

Heaven is creation and existence. Without the heavens/space, there wouldn't be a canvas for stars, solar systems, or other universes to have been formed. The creative is the embodiment of Tao (the way) forever moving and creating; the will of God (universal life force). It is now and forever ceaseless, tireless, and moving forward endless and generative. The creative heaven is an oracle of possibilities; beginning with knowing and acknowledging that we are and have been a possibility. Think of the probability of our existence, think of the supernatural occurrence of this solar system manifesting Earth. Let Earth be the divine proof of all things seen and unseen that can be made possible. In essence, if we are possible (life on earth humans etc.) that everything else that you might not believe in is possible. The creative emphasizes you being here and now forever moving forward adapting, failing, and correcting yourself. This can be extended to acknowledging our journey from life to death and back to life. This is the profound oracle of the I Ching that pronounces the existence of the universal life force which was not denied (Tao or will of God) and that's the way it is. For those that accept it wonderful, for those that do not, it is not in their time to do so. In essence, they are not there yet. Ask yourself? Are you there yet? Because this sign expresses that no matter how far you've come, and how far you think you are to go, there is always more. Hence, don't try so hard to tire yourself, but

allow yourself to get there, especially if it is right. This is an oracle were pushing forward and staying on the path leads to success. Hence, to persevere, perseverance takes you further. Oracle of creativity and the strength to move forward despite adversities. Although, it's always best to move in the direction of least resistance. Also, moving forward staying on path means, that the shortest distance between two points is to stay on a straight path. To know your direction and not deviate nor zigzag, because indecisions will slow you down and be a waste of time. This oracle prescribes being in harmony with heaven i.e., spirituality, religious inclinations, or practices. To act correctly and in moderation. To move carefully and be aware of dangers and surroundings. Honor, respect, and integrity are keen to succeed; be generous, kind, look to improve yourself, and influence others in positive ways. One must remain loyal and never betray those that support and serve you. To remain humble, let go of ego, pride, and prejudices. To know how to begin things and carry plans, ideas, and aspirations through to fruition. This oracle recommends not being arrogant; never boasting, bragging, or thinking yourself better than others. Not to harm or do evil to anyone. Never take advantage of others or those deemed weaker. But, to prove one's worth in being a symbol of hope, mutual respect of others, supporting those in their walks of life to find their purpose. But most of all, you find your purpose and reason for being. In this way, others and you can achieve happiness in knowing that your life has meant something.

Internal Tetragram Geomancy Code

1
1
1
0

I Ching tetragram 02 - Corruption; Yoruba Cowrie 03 - Ogunda;
Yoruba IFa Ogunda

This is an oracle of being dedicated to a profession, as well
as safeguarding your position, title, work, or livelihood. It's to
avoid putting your freedom at risk i.e., justice situation. Avoid
putting your life at risk through physical altercations, or
quarreling. It's an oracle of fights, violence, stealing, or desiring a
big score; in essence, beware of desiring to obtain things through
force or illegal means. Never take advantage of the weak, mistreat
others, or you'll suffer being mistreated. Someone needs
protection against justice situations or help in winning a court
case, or battle in general. Beware of injury working with tools,
vehicles, accidents due to stress or over working. Oracle of having
strength but knowing when and how to use it. Wasted strength
depletes and turns into a weakness. One needs to be tenderer
and earn the respect of mates and others through kindness.
Ogunda teaches us that war is necessary for peace to reign in the
end. But everything doesn't have to be a battle when you can win
with wisdom. The greatest asset of Ogunda is to become
educated, acquiring skills, or recognizing one's talent and profiting

from it. This is an oracle of creating, inventing, constructing, building, and engineering. Learn, especially about what tools you will need that can support your talents or make your life easier. Oracle of work, and making oneself useful, not useless.

HEXAGRAM

29

29 Danger Abysmal Water

      This oracle states that there is a river or ocean to cross. Oracle of exposing oneself to danger, liking the excitement of it, or did not account for it after a decision that was made. When things are handled correctly, crossing a river or great ocean of affairs can be met with success. What is needed is bravery and the loss of fear. The will to meet challenges with honesty and sincerity. A person's attitude, character, and behavior must be well aligned with what is being experienced. Negativity doesn't hide, it is everywhere, can be caused, or shows up at any time. Noticing it before it can get hold of your environment helps plan for a circumvention intervention. This means to have ample time to set in motions decisions that will support not getting into a predicament. We need to recognize when to push forward, as with when not too. If one is too anxious or restless? Things might not go well unless one relaxes or takes a step back for a moment. Admit when help or support is needed to lessen the stressor and support a positive transition. Taking precautions supports being in control and not allowing for situations to get worse. Always know that there are consequences to wrongful acts, and sooner or later everyone gets caught in some way or another.

Internal Hexagram

27 The Corners of the Mouth

There are good reasons for opening one's mouth, and other reasons for keeping it shut.
This oracle says that we can tell a lot about individuals by what they nourish themselves with. There are those that nourish the belly, those that nourish the mind, those that nourish their bodies, those that nourish spirituality, and those only desire to nourish tongues with gossip and falsehoods. In essence, too much of anything is not good, as in we need a balance even when it comes to what we decide to nourish ourselves with. Food can enter the mouth tasting very good, yet leave the body smelling foul, as in it decays within the digestive system. When is something good for you and when is something just not right or no longer of good taste? We must look around and seek the truths, speak truths, and discern lies. When do certain people or situations cease to provide something that is of worth, useful, and tangible. Actions can cease to be of worth when they don't provide something of value, as in when they hurt others. This is an oracle of working on physical, emotional, psychological, and spiritual well-being, not stigmatization, discrimination, stereotyping, or giving in to hate and prejudices.

0
0
1
0

I Ching tetragram 14 - Purity; Yoruba Cowrie 12 - Eyila; Yoruba IFa Otrupon

Otrupon is to be offended, to offend, or someone is on the offensive. Implying the need to protect yourself. This is an oracle of overcoming traumas; bullied, violated, disrespected, embarrassed, harassed, assaulted, cursed out, or abused. Speaks of wanting out of a relation, situation, job, and unable to find the way out. There is someone that wants to take over or win everything at all costs. They would do w1hatever it takes to get someone out of their way and obtain their means. Not to give in to selfishness, ego, or pride; also, to never be prejudice, misjudge, nor persecute anyone unjustly. Speaks of family betraying one another. Where mates in a separation battle over possessions and custody to the brinks of destroying one another. After a storm comes to calm as in - we need to weather storms; know how to outlive ordeals. Otrupon is an oracle of peace and harmony returning after having undergone situations of great turmoil and tribulation. With Otrupon one must be very intelligent not to lose while trying to be slicker than the rest. Hence, not to be overconfident in thinking you are getting over on others. As the same, beware of someone desiring to get over on you in some fashion and gain leverage or advantage over a situation. In this oracle, folks easily forgot the sacrifices that you make for those you love. Hence, folks forget the sacrifices one makes for others in general. Don't be the same lead by example be the better person, but always cover your butt.

HEXAGRAM

30

30 The Clinging Fire Enlightenment

In this hexagram we look for enlightenment, the proper way of thinking, and awakened knowledge. Great clarity in vision thought and understanding leads to success. This can be through studying, reading to keep informed, or the desire to always learn. Clinging also implies aligning oneself to those that can give guidance and mentorship. Once enlightenment is attained, we can now be of use and spread that enlightenment guiding and teaching others. In essence, helping those acquire awareness. This sign also is one of obtaining, like fire needs wood for continued light, sustenance, and generating energy. We too need something that can supply us with the proper fuel to keep things moving, especially in the right direction. The advice is to also be mindful of not doing things that will corrupt or endanger the clarity of your enlightenment, otherwise danger ensues, and the fire burns out, or goes wild becoming chaos.

28

28 - Preponderance of the Great - Excessiveness or Extra

Oracle of excessiveness, extra, too much to handle, or overindulging. This also means too beware of gluttony, greed, or exaggeration. The advice is to understand when something is too much, overkill, or know when something is being overdone. Something will break when it is in excess, it stresses that all things must be handled correctly and with care for what things to not break. Proper due diligence (homework), evaluations, and executions will give way to successful outcome. Excess, or extra is good when it meets expectations or surpasses them. Preponderance of the great also means to accept change or know that change is unavoidable no matter how much we try to push forward or hold back. The individual might want to but forces more powerful are pushing for things to manifest despite of attempting to control them.

1
1
0
1

I Ching tetragram 03 - Activities; Yoruba Cowrie 13 - Metanla; Yoruba IFa Irete

Irete is an oracle of being sought after looked for or found. Beware of investigations, or being probed, and getting caught. Irete represents escaping, an escape, climbing out of a hole/ditch, or getting out of a rut. When desperate or in despair there will be someone or a situation will arise that will give way to the needed support in overcoming the difficulty. Irete is an oracle of upward mobility as in stepping up a ladder or striving towards bettering oneself, rising above the rest, or rising to the occasion. It is one of undergoing physical challenges, beware of early disease or injuries to one's limbs via falling and fracturing. Also beware of accidents, not being mindful. When it comes to women this is a sign that relates to difficult pregnancies. In general, beware of love triangles and promiscuity, which can lead to STDs. Learning how to attend to spirit guides and ancestors is important because it's a sign that marks communications with them. Learn to be obedient and listen to ancestral advice. There will be a reunion or gathering soon. The person needs much love, romanticism, and finding the correct mate to ensure happiness. This is not

something that happens trying too hard. It's something the happens being at the right place and right time. In Irete religious activities are much more favorable to the person's energy than social ones (partying).

HEXAGRAM

31

31 - Influence

Oracle of the proper influence or influenza for the right things to transpire. In this hexagram individuals need to influence one another in a positive way by knowing how to relate to each other. With proper behavior, free of prejudices, and being indiscriminate with respect all things resolve favorably. People need to like each other for influence, wooing, or swaying to occur; otherwise, there will be rejection. Folks need to know when someone can be influenced and when they cannot be. Listening to the right advice can be a positive influence towards making good decisions. Avoiding trying to influence someone that is difficult to please or rejects you will lead to embarrassment. Never use swaying for control, domination, or manipulative intentions because it does backfire.

44

44 - Coming to Meet, Coupling, Meeting

People meet to discuss, brainstorm, or deliver a message. This can be a friendly hang out, business meeting, seductive meetup/getting to know each other, sexual encounters11, or dangerous hidden agenda. This sign focuses on knowing that there is or will be a meeting of some sort. That you are to be or keep in control relative to the kind of meeting this is and never allow for any situation to become negative or dangerous. To always be aware of person's behaviors, attitudes, and intentions. This recommends preparation for the meeting and thinking of all possible outcomes to the meeting, so there are no surprises. Know that all persons gathering are aligned with each other's motives for the meeting. If it is contractual or in competition look to leverage i.e., to be at an advantage point. If it's a one to one, think of the possibility of what they are trying to accomplish and how? Beware of false illusions or talking a good game for the sake of persuasion. Always be mindful, or conscientious of who's influencing who.

1
1
0
0

I Ching tetragram 03 - Enthusiasm; Yoruba Cowrie 04 - Iroso;
Yoruba IFa Iroso

Iroso means the unknown, mysterious, hidden, secrets, and surprises. This is a sign of riches, obtaining, inheriting, or achieving status. It's to avoid entrapments of being made part of a grander scheme. Iroso has a saying, "No one knows the mysteries that lie beneath the depths of the seas." As in a blessing, which can come out of nowhere; as well as trouble when taken in a negative context. It's an oracle of discovery as much as it is of exposure to danger. It announces a business takeover or b1eing taken advantage of. It recommends avoiding risky business to minimize losses or ending up catching a court case. It marks life coming to an end regarding a terminal illness or having a short life due to lifestyle choices. The person needs to work diligently with the divinities and ancestors to avoid anger issues, heart disease, or other sudden incidentals due to living a stressful life. This is an oracle of avoiding being crooked or influenced by criminal elements or intentions. Iroso is an oracle of traps being laid, hidden agendas, extortion, or blackmail. "If you can't do the time, then don't do the crime." If you like an adrenaline rush and

exposing yourself and others to danger, then be ready to pay for the consequences of those actions. Beware of someone desiring to get rid of you from somewhere, removing, or getting you out of the way for them to take over. Oracle of being let go, fired or no longer desired.

HEXAGRAM

32

32 - Duration Enduring Perpetuation

A good example of positive duration or something perpetual is a marriage. When people join in ritual matrimony it's; "as long as we live, and till death do we part." This is an example of desiring something endures. There is positive perpetuation and negative perpetuations. Negatives are predicaments that we get into that seem to never end, such as a bad favor that leaves one stuck to an obligation or responsibility that's not yours. For durations to be positive both parties need to have a vested interest in supporting and solidifying the relationship or situation. We must strengthen each other and be in the same mindset. Moving in opposite directions is contrary to positive duration. In unity there is strength as with divided in goals and aspirations we'll fall.

43

43 Resoluteness Breakthrough

This is the moment of seeing things through, resolving, or catching a break. Speaks of overcoming negative people, situations, or those that wish to keep one down. This oracle teaches to never try to resolve situations using force, when possible, but to win through small progressive advancement that might not be noticed by the enemies or obstructionist. Being aware of dangers and resisting the temptation of meeting it heads on. It is never a sign of weakness to ask for support or seek allies. This oracle's advice to never exhaust yourself trying too hard to overcome something. Negatives have a tendency of weakening and they're lies the opportunity to advance. Patience is necessary for breakthrough because all it takes is the right moment.

1
1
1
0

I Ching tetragram 02 - Corruption; Yoruba Cowrie 03 - Ogunda;
Yoruba IFa Ogunda

This is an oracle of being dedicated to a profession, as well as safeguarding your position, title, work, or livelihood. It's to avoid putting your freedom at risk i.e., justice situation. Avoid putting your life at risk through physical altercations, or quarreling. It's an oracle of fights, violence, stealing, or desiring a big score; in essence, beware of desiring to obtain things through force or illegal means. Never take advantage of the weak, mistreat others, or you'll suffer being mistreated. Someone needs protection against justice situations or help in winning a court case, or battle in general. Beware of injury working with tools, vehicles, accidents due to stress or over working. Oracle of having strength but knowing when and how to use it. Wasted strength depletes and turns into a weakness. One needs to be tenderer and earn the respect of mates and others through kindness. Ogunda teaches us that war is necessary for peace to reign in the end. But everything doesn't have to be a battle when you can win with wisdom. The greatest asset of Ogunda is to become educated, acquiring skills, or recognizing one's talent and profiting

from it. This is an oracle of creating, inventing, constructing, building, and engineering. Learn, especially about what tools you will need that can support your talents or make your life easier. Oracle of work, and making oneself useful, not useless.

HEXAGRAM

33 - Retreat Retiring

This is the oracle of taking a step back. Most might look at retiring or retreat as giving up. But that's not the case, it recommends taking a break. It's a pause to analyze and reflect before on situations before plunging forward rash, spontaneous, or overzealously. The act of retreating is something that should be done calculatedly and being reserved. People don't need to know the strategy behind you take a step back. One doesn't retreat in defeat but intelligently because it is necessary. This is one of the best moves or things to do in a time of uncertainty or conflict.

44 - Coming to Meet, Coupling, Meeting

People meet to discuss, brainstorm, or deliver a message. This can be a friendly hang out, business meeting, seductive meetup/getting to know each other, sexual encounters, or dangerous hidden agenda. This sign focuses on knowing that there is or will be a meeting of some sort. That you are to be or keep in control relative to the kind of meeting this is and never allow for any situation to become negative or dangerous. To always be aware of person's behaviors, attitudes, and intentions. This recommends preparation for the meeting and thinking of all possible outcomes to the meeting, so there are no surprises. Know that all persons gathering are aligned with each other's motives for the meeting. If it is contractual or in competition look to leverage i.e., to be at an advantage point. If it's a one to one, think of the possibility of what they are trying to accomplish and how? Beware of false illusions or talking a good game for the sake of persuasion. Always be mindful, or conscientious of who's influencing who.

Internal Tetragram Geomancy Code

1
1
0
0

I Ching tetragram 03 - Enthusiasm; Yoruba Cowrie 04 - Iroso;
Yoruba IFa Iroso

     Iroso means the unknown, mysterious, hidden, secrets,
and surprises. This is a sign of riches, obtaining, inheriting, or
achieving status. It's to avoid entrapments of being made part of a
grander scheme. Iroso has a saying, "No one knows the mysteries
that lie beneath the depths of the seas." As in a blessing, which
can come out of nowhere; as well as trouble when taken in a
negative context. It's an oracle of discovery as much as it is of
exposure to danger. It announces a business takeover or being
taken advantage of. It recommends avoiding risky business to
minimize losses or ending up catching a court case. It marks life
coming to an end regarding a terminal illness or having a short life
due to lifestyle choices. The person needs to work diligently with
the divinities and ancestors to avoid anger issues, heart disease,
or other sudden incidentals due to living a stressful life. This is an
oracle of avoiding being crooked or influenced by criminal
elements or intentions. Iroso is an oracle of traps being laid,
hidden agendas, extortion, or blackmail. "If you can't do the time,
then don't do the crime." If you like an adrenaline rush and

exposing yourself and others to danger, then be ready to pay for the consequences of those actions. Beware of someone desiring to get rid of you from somewhere, removing, or getting you out of the way for them to take over. Oracle of being let go, fired or no longer desired.

HEXAGRAM

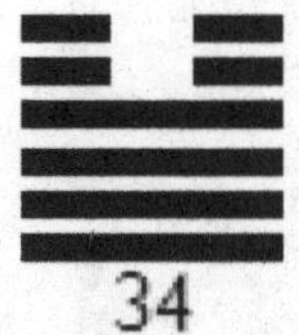

34 - The Power of the Great / Great Strength

The key to great strength is control. As in technique wins over brute strength. Hence, the use of intelligence to conserve strength, and use strength to empower because it is necessary. This demands patience for the right moment to use strength to its optimum advantage. Power needs to be measured and initiated carefully from a position of calm and least resistance rather than when in motion. From calm there is a burst, as opposed to motion requiring a recoil. In essence, the use of strength intelligently rather than without thinking, which can cause harm or nonproductive. Strength is better used while keeping things organized, orderly, consistent, and steadfast. Appropriate strength is not stubborn nor inflexible but measured and secure.

Internal hexagram

43 Resoluteness Breakthrough

This is the moment of seeing things through, resolving, or catching a break. Speaks of overcoming negative people, situations, or those that wish to keep one down. This oracle teaches to never try to resolve situations using force, when possible, but to win through small progressive advancement that might not be noticed by the enemies or obstructionist. Being aware of dangers and resisting the temptation of meeting it heads on. It is never a sign of weakness to ask for support or seek allies. This oracle's advice to never exhaust yourself trying too hard to overcome something. Negatives have a tendency of weakening and they're lies the opportunity to advance. Patience is necessary for breakthrough because all it takes is the right moment.

1
1
1
1

I Ching tetragram 01 - Voyage; Yoruba Cowrie 08 - Eyeunle;
Yoruba IFa Ogbe

Ogbe is the oracle of consciousness and will. So, you think so you are, where your mind takes you, so there will you be. From a positive point of view, it's where one becomes proud of one's achievements or how far one has come/traveled. It's to be on track with achieving goals and to see things through. On a negative thought, once you've felt that you've reached the top, then the worst that can happen is to suffer a fall or loss. This is an oracle of going through separations and adaptation to change; especially after making decisions that take you in the wrong direction. It advises not to lose your head i.e., give in to negative ego, or impulses. It recommends patience and protective actions. If your time is up where you are, then it's time to move on; life is not just one journey, but a long road that never ends. Speaking in this oracle are all situations dealing with the mind, thoughts, knowledge, understanding, wisdom, and ignorance. Not thinking properly will lead to confrontations, and one must beware of never overstepping boundaries. Support unity, but if needing to separate do so without violence. Know that all endings lead to

new beginnings. Beware of actions that can turn into a justice situation, or lawsuit. But most of all to be organized or bringing order to your life. This is an oracle of being saved by taking a leap of faith and entering some form of spiritual practice. Ogbe is also, road, path, and to be elevated to a new position. There is a tendency towards being or becoming narcissistic, selfish, and not empathic to others, i.e., arrogance and ignorance can lead to this. In essence, not to see through the eyes of others, or feel their concerns. It's not all about you, you affect others, and others you. Having bad behavior is imposing one's will to the extreme of not caring who they step on or who they injure along the way. It's there way or the highway; consequences to actions is sometimes overlooked when it comes to obtaining their means. One must be careful to bite more than one can chew. Things done by force will be met with contention and conflicts will follow. This is a mighty oracle announces blessings and successes that are to be achieved in ones' life. But, only through intelligence, wisdom, patience, and honorable means. All that can be supported by the will of God, and positive divinities in the right way.

HEXAGRAM

35

35 - Progress

As the name implies Progress, to progress, or advance. If an individual is honorable, just, and virtuous progress is on the rise. When one is in line with the energy of progress the difficulty is in maintaining and extending it. Ask how hard it was to obtain or being in a position of progress? Now, contemplate on how complicated it can be to keep it. The advice is to keep away from distractions, inferior choices, or bad decision making. Self-analysis and self-awareness of dangers will always support continued progress. Also, not to be denial of what or where potential dangers are so as your progress doesn't fall short. Finally, not to be afraid of asking for support, this too, will help maintain or take progress to another level. When things seem to backfire a bit during progress, the recommendation is to not give up. Push forward because this is a time of progress, perseverance favors you.

Internal Hexagram

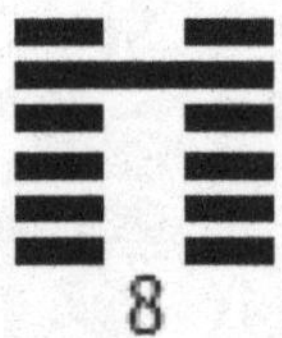

08 Holding Together

Can you hold things together, keep it together, or keep those together that are necessary for things to be successful? This is an oracle of things not getting out of hand. Things cannot be disorganized or in disarray. If this is the case proper planning has suffered and upon execution (trying to get things done) situations will not hold. It is important to have vision, foresight, and stay ten steps ahead of situations for things to be held together. Where can you see that there is a loose link a weakness within or surroundings that merits attention. Holding together is to tighten up.

1
0
0
0

I Ching tetragram 08 - Authority; Yoruba Cowrie 06 - Obara;
Yoruba IFa Obara

Obara says, "There can't be changed without revolution -
chaos or torment." An oracle of wisdom, intelligence, and learning
how to better live or coexist with those in your environment.
Business related relative to marketing and knowing how to deliver
goods to markets. The market rises, and the markets fall. It's
where wheels turn/move forward, but there are times when we
need to turn back or go backwards. Obara is an oracle where
being proud leads to starvation, being left alone, or being put to
the side. Oracle of success or failure, where the tongue, verb, or
speaking can save you or do you in. The tongue can be used for
evil, as it can be used for good. Good when it's used to praise,
pray for good things, and bless. Evil went it's used to offend, false
witness, and lie. So, mind your tongue. Speaks of knowing how to
stay standing up and not falling after having worked hard in
obtaining a position or move up in life. Speaks of good business
relations when fair. Speaks of difficulties in maintaining
relationships (personal, social) due to being difficult to satisfy. In
Obara one needs to maintain focus on education and utilizing

one's talents or gifts to become successful. One is not to allow matters of the heart, emotions, or promiscuity to get in the way of one's success. Concentration and focus on achievements will bring happiness and many positive things. Giving in to pettiness, childishness, egotism, and distractions will lead to failure. The individual from a young age must learn to discern lies, and not fall into anti-social behavior. This will inevitably lead to doom. This is an oracle of planning, setting goals, and knowing how to execute the plan. Oracle of conquering and escaping danger when knowing how not to be in the wrong place, and at the wrong time. This is an oracle of not being a liar, learning that there is no honor in lying.

HEXAGRAM

36

36 - The Darkening of the Light

This signifies situations not being favorable or not going your way. This encompasses encountering an arbitrary force, obstacle, or unforeseen circumstance. The advice is to not force your way out of this period, but to use this time for assessing and replanning. Negative situations, frustrations, or hard times are eventually followed by a great achievement or bounce back. Whether hit with an economic loss, illness, injury, or betrayal that leaves one incapacitated for a bit. The time can still be put to good use. The execution of a plan after getting back on track is necessary for continued success. Going through and ordeal or hardship should give one experience for future contingency planning. So, if one foresees the potential for a negative recurring, there is a plan in place to overcome it. Henceforth, avoiding hitting rock bottom again.

07 - The Army

What is the Army or an Army? It is organization and leadership. Without a formation or structure an army is easily combated. Army teaches us that we need to count on superiors with intelligence and not try to take on tasks ourselves; knowing we need leadership and guidance. An army can only be successful as, is its strategy. And this comes from the minds of it is leaders. Individuals must ask themselves if they have what it takes to gather the right group of individuals, that are up to the task of leading. Is its leader worthy of respect, integrity, and honor and merit others to follow them? The oracle emphasizes not going to battle alone. An Army from a spiritual perspective, points to obtaining guidance from spirit guides, ancestors, or divine masters - that one is connected too. Learn to communicate with them, especially when unable to count on people.

0
1
0
1

I Ching tetragram 11 - Limitations; Yoruba Cowrie 10 - Ofun;
Yoruba IFa Ofun

Ofun is an oracle of self-defense, where defending yourself
is permitted. It's an oracle of great wisdom, growth, and
grandeur. Yet, not to allow the grandeur to get one's head, or it
will cause failures and setbacks. This oracle stresses seeking
perfection and balance. In essence, greatness without humility or
not knowing limitations will lead to demise and destruction. This
oracle personifies living in harmony with society, nature, and your
surroundings - Tao. It's where God's messengers/holy
scriptures/words and testaments enter the world to teach
mankind how to better live. Signifies losing one's life accidentally,
or by mistake. Oracle recommends never overstepping one's
position, being disobedient, taking unnecessary risk, or imposing
will on others. This is an oracle of understanding boundaries,
limitations, and knowing which lines are never too cross. What
comes to mind with this oracle is "You're only as strong as the
next person, which is equal to you or stronger." Ofun is an oracle
of recognizing we can't know everything; we can't have
everything, and we will lose thinking we are everything. Beware of

stepping out of line with one's actions or misjudging individuals. Oracle of being mindful of one's actions and the consequences that they can cause, as well as the actions of others along the same lines. With this oracle we learn to understand the nature of death. As in the cycle of a disease individual that slowly deteriorates leading to death. This cycle includes the individual and family coping with the process, beginning with denial, anger, anxiety, depression, acceptance, and finally grief. The spiritual process begins with death (reapers) coming to meet, hopefully in a controlled way, but as we know death can be sudden too. Then, the crossing over, extends to family acknowledging their ancestors, and initiating spiritual practices for the transcendence of their souls. Ofun represents processes involving the land of the dead, working with the dead, elevation or crossing over of the dead through ancestor worship.

HEXAGRAM

37 Family or Group

Blood is thicker than water, and everyone in a family carry mutual traits. Hence, in a family folks must strive towards getting along. Getting along with your family is like getting along with oneself. This is attributed to all members recognizing each other's roles and position; know yourself and what you can contribute to the whole. This begins with a good leader that can motivate and inspire others as well as keep the family organized and intact. All members must maintain good character in meeting individual goals. The family or group is a collective. This means that all have separate responsibilities, but when putting them all together working in common interest, they accomplish optimum goals. Recognition must be given especially to those that have or share in the task of keeping everyone together. In relation to an actual family, one should ask if one believes in family, and if you do, will it require a marriage. Always remember that when forging a family, it becomes something greater than oneself. A family is a legacy, so nothing should be thought of in short term. Legacies are meant to exist long past our existence and withstand the test of generations.

64

64 Before Completion

One can never be overzealous in starting a new venture, when one has not fully completed the previous one. This is an oracle of cross checking and marking things along the way as they complete. Ask yourself what is missing to complete? Then, take things from there. Things cannot be accomplished before its time, or until all work or job is done. This is true in all phases of transition, change, or new things to come. There is a proper way of bringing closure and that is not being careless. Admit when somethings are not ready, and incomplete to bring closure. Holding back or showing restraint is not a bad thing. It's better to be sure than doubtful, or better to be safe than sorry. Also, just because you can sense or feel the completion and it's within grasp, doesn't mean to relax. Cross checking requires being meticulous.

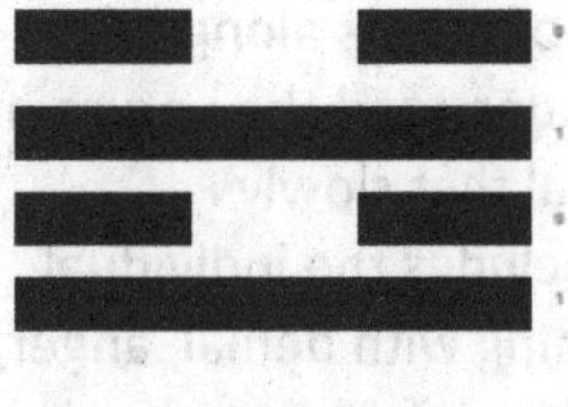

0
1
0
1

I Ching tetragram 11 - Limitations; Yoruba Cowrie 10 - Ofun; Yoruba IFa Ofun

Ofun is an oracle of self-defense, where defending yourself is permitted. It's an oracle of great wisdom, growth, and grandeur. Yet, not to allow the grandeur to get one's head, or it will cause failures and setbacks. This oracle stresses seeking perfection and balance. In essence, greatness without humility or not knowing limitations will lead to demise and destruction. This oracle personifies living in harmony with society, nature, and your surroundings - Tao. It's where God's messengers/holy scriptures/words and testaments enter the world to teach mankind how to better live. Signifies losing one's life accidentally, or by mistake. Oracle recommends never overstepping one's position, being disobedient, taking unnecessary risk, or imposing will on others. This is an oracle of understanding boundaries, limitations, and knowing which lines are never too cross. What comes to mind with this oracle is "You're only as strong as the next person, which is equal to you or stronger." Ofun is an oracle of recognizing we can't know everything; we can't have everything, and we will lose thinking we are everything. Beware of

stepping out of line with one's actions or misjudging individuals. Oracle of being mindful of one's actions and the consequences that they can cause, as well as the actions of others along the same lines. With this oracle we learn to understand the nature of death. As in the cycle of a disease individual that slowly deteriorates leading to death. This cycle includes the individual and family coping with the process, beginning with denial, anger, anxiety, depression, acceptance, and finally grief. The spiritual process begins with death (reapers) coming to meet, hopefully in a controlled way, but as we know death can be sudden too. Then, the crossing over, extends to family acknowledging their ancestors, and initiating spiritual practices for the transcendence of their souls. Ofun represents processes involving the land of the dead, working with the dead, elevation or crossing over of the dead through ancestor worship.

HEXAGRAM

38 Opposition

When opposition arrives, one needs to be diligent and advance slowly, not rush, nor push forward spontaneously. This is a time where someone, or something does not blend, mix, unite, and goes against others. Know that when people oppose one another problems will arise. Hence, meeting each other halfway in small matters can lead to better things or problem solving. Look at the benefits of resolving a little bit at a time and make changes that can bring about a positive outcome, even when there is opposition. Finger pointing, arguments, and stubbornness won't solve anything. Coming to terms due to mutual respect and using diplomacy will set things back on track and all will benefit.

63

63 After Completion, Completed

This oracle signifies taking a break after completing tasks, ventures, assignments, or milestone achievement. This is a time to get reorganized for the next plan or strategy that needs execution. The break is for a visualization of the future an outreach mental assessment of what is to follow. Physical labor does not need to be included at this time just the brainstorming that leads to proper organization of ideas. It is also forward thinking for clarity in direction in way things should go and staying ahead. The oracle advises to completely resolve all outstanding issues, so that any new venture can begin on a clean slate. Never carry old baggage to new situations, you will be contaminating it, in essence extending what should have been complete. This defeats the purpose of starting something new.

1
0
1
1

I Ching tetragram 05 - Grace; Yoruba Cowrie 16 - Meridilogun;
Yoruba IFa Otura

Otura speaks of living in an inhospitable place. It's to be surrounded or live among con artists, and thieves. Also, to avoid being conned or tricked, someone is to be outwitted. Never be the first to know or know the most and the last to take advantage of opportunities. This is a sign of not being given recognition for your efforts or taken for granted. Don't take things for granted, life, family, relationship, jobs, or career, etc. Oracle of being too slow to take advantage of an opportunity due to being distracted. The person needs to have a sharp mind and keep things in order. Not saying you are going to do but doing it, especially with honor. The sooner an individual acquires the necessary skills, and identifies their talents or career, the sooner they will be successful. Oracle prescribes not allowing situations to drag. Bringing closure to situations will allow for one to go on to the next thing without skipping a beat. This sign doesn't permit delaying because carelessness and making mistakes will take hold. Oracle of knowing how to live within your means, respect, and worships the forces of God. How well and proficient individual

works with the divine forces, so will their grace bring them blessings. Speaks of dark forces robbing the person's luck, happiness, and economic well-being when not appeased or expunged in time. Yet, Otura is an oracle of resolving with good luck when situations are taken care of in time. Identify grace, gift, or being gracious in doing things with good taste, will win the hearts of others. And, with this comes the necessary support, not being alone, or left alone with all the weight upon your shoulders.

HEXAGRAM

39

39 Obstruction Hesitation

To be obstructed is to be blocked, held back, or not allowed to move forward. There are moments that this is due to the environment or timing. Time meaning year, month, day, season, or moment. There are positive seasons and negative ones. We can't always have things our way. Identify where the obstruction is coming from and formulate a plan for getting out of the way of what is blocking or understand that it can unblock itself. There are times in which we need the advice of someone wiser that can help us see how to remove the obstruction. Then, there are times where we need to hesitate or obstruct things for ourselves to avoid a foreseen danger. Hence, stop evaluate whether some situation was a bad choice, or mistake that is being caught on time. All deliberate hesitation or holding back will conclude with the correct decision as too when to move forward again. Hopefully, by then one has a better plan to execute.

64

64 Before Completion

One can never be overzealous in starting a new venture, when one has not fully completed the previous one. This is an oracle of cross checking and marking things along the way as they complete. Ask yourself what is missing to complete? Then, take things from there. Things cannot be accomplished before its time, or until all work or job is done. This is true in all phases of transition, change, or new things to come. There is a proper way of bringing closure and that is not being careless. Admit when somethings are not ready, and incomplete to bring closure. Holding back or showing restraint is not a bad thing. It's better to be sure than doubtful, or better to be safe than sorry. Also, just because you can sense or feel the completion and it's within grasp, doesn't mean to relax. Cross checking requires being meticulous.

Internal Tetragram Geomancy Code

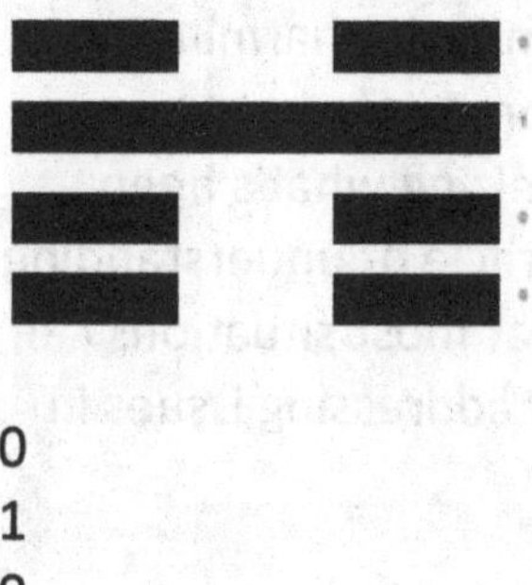

0
1
0
0

I Ching tetragram 12 - Violation; Yoruba Cowrie 14 - Merinla;
Yoruba IFa Ika

    Ika means to know how to get around situations. It is an oracle of finding the correct approach to things. One needs to find themselves, and their correct way of being. But most importantly stability in life, i.e., where or what brings stability. If the individual has been kicked out, lost their job/home, their stability? They will need to help in getting back on track. Look to spirituality for this support or find those that can give guidance and ritual work to bring you back from the loss. Ika is an oracle of going to battle, or having to battle, along with the work that is needed to win. It's where we as young folks hit the road of life in a direction towards finding our profession, place, position, where one is going to be successful. If you find yourself struggling to much and going through obstacles and hard times. This is a definite indicator that you are not where you need to be. Ika is an oracle of avoiding battles or getting out them. Avoid spiritual battles with folks that utilize spirituality to do harm. Suggest too, allow elders or more experienced people to help you through guidance; don't try to be a know it all. Ika is an oracle of helping others and through

goodwill unto others, returning favors or someone least expected help you when most needed occurs. Hence, one is not to reject help due to pride. This is an oracle of the family not harming one another. Beware of being kicked out your home, job, work, relationship, or someplace due to not recognizing what's been going on. In essence you snooze you lose. Oracle of understanding what is evident or inevitable. Understand that most situations can be resolved just by getting out of the way or addressing issues in time.

HEXAGRAM

40

40 Deliverance Release

    Anytime one releases tension, stress, or is released from being enslaved/imprisoned is a good thing. This is to be delivered, may we be delivered from or out of all negative situations and intent. Have deliverance is to be liberated, untangled, and unbound. There are bindings that are unnecessary, unneeded, and difficult to get out of. Recognize when you are putting yourself into an unpleasant situation binding to something that doesn't provide a blessing. This is an oracle of having a good outcome relative to being set free. It points to having been or being disturbed bothered, or unwillingly attached, even by mistake. There is nothing better than freedom. Hence, if you need to let someone go do so, for everyone's happiness. Selfishness, and control for the sake of egotism and stubbornness will never bring success in the end. They're many things that we must let go or let be free.

63

63 After Completion, Completed

This oracle signifies taking a break after completing tasks, ventures, assignments, or milestone achievement. This is a time to get reorganized for the next plan or strategy that needs execution. The break is for a visualization of the future an outreach mental assessment of what is to follow. Physical labor does not need to be included at this time just the brainstorming that leads to proper organization of ideas. It is also forward thinking for clarity in direction in way things should go and staying ahead. The oracle advises to completely resolve all outstanding issues, so that any new venture can begin on a clean slate. Never carry old baggage to new situations, you will be contaminating it, in essence extending what should have been complete. This defeats the purpose of starting something new.

1
0
1
0

I Ching tetragram 06 - Dissolution; Yoruba Cowrie 05 - Oche;
Yoruba IFa Oche

Oracle of the blood being thicker than water, blood being the transporter of cells for living organisms to function. In essence, blood is life. Oracle where money came into the world, and today is the lifeblood of society, business, commerce, or government economies. This is an oracle of fights over money, and in some cases over livelihood (bringing food to your table). Oracle of being cheated or feeling cheated. It's the oracle where the money is cursed, or "the root to all evil." Human blood feeds money i.e., the blood sweat, and tears of those that work to survive. Rich folks curse it because many of them don't want to lose it. Poor folks curse it because they don't have it, and it eludes them. In Oche negativity stems from the decomposition of things, corruption, failures, when situations fall apart. Uncleanliness, impurities, or filthiness corrupts and generates diseases. Hence, sanitize, wash, purify, and never allow germs, parasites, or viruses to take hold. Taking care of one's digestion, and blood is important to avoid illnesses or diseases from an early age. Oche is an oracle of dysfunctional, disorganized family, relationships, or

affairs. The protection of the family, economic position, and not allowing for relationship problems getting in the way of happiness is key to being successful. In this oracle one is to make one's spirituality stronger through dedication, devotion, and being responsible with one's gift; otherwise, one loses the gift and gives way to the decomposition of all things. Oche is an oracle of protecting that which you've worked so hard to maintain. Love God and his divinities so you attend them, so will they support you in getting out of situations and resolving for better living. Oche is an oracle of needing to be saved through taking a leap of faith and entering a shamanistic priestly way of life.

HEXAGRAM

41

41 Decrease Reducing

A time of decrease or a time for decrease. Going through a decrease can be forced or planned. We downsize or decrease because it is intelligent to do so before things get worse. This type of planned decrease gives way to future success because one is setting up for a time where gains will be possible again. Forced decrease are a consequence of mistakes, miscalculation, improper planning that led towards taking a potential loss. This oracle states that one does not gain anything from getting angry or upset. One should understand the frustrations associated with the errors and correct them as soon as possible. This will diminish the amount of decrease or fall one must take. Never be too proud, or ashamed to ask for support or counsel on ways to fix situations. No one is perfect and the sooner one turns things around the better things will be.

Internal Hexagram

19 Approach

The correct angle to things. Approach is to align or find the proper order of execution to situations. The right course of action, or choices in tasks and agreements that lead to mutual benefit to all parties. Because the wrong approach will bring about failure and having to start over. Careful, intelligent approach with support of others leads to success. Negative attitudes or character will not contribute to the right approach on the contrary, it will delay and disenchant the undertaking.

0
0
1
1

I Ching tetragram 13 - Success; Yoruba Cowrie 11 - Ojuani; Yoruba IFa Ojuani

Ojuani means from riches to rags, and from rags to riches. It's an oracle of doubts, complexes, and potential insecurities. Persons have an overzealous ambition that when not held back can become destructive. Oracle where person's must keep their ego in check. Learn to live with others in peace strive for an education obtaining a career profession, or title. To be a responsible and not a careless individual, beware of desires; we can't have everything or everything we think is good for us might not be. Oracle of becoming easily bored with mates, so beware of promiscuity and STDs. People lose due to jealousy, and envy within a circle of friendships, work, and even family. Speaks of dark forces getting in the way of progress, external or internal. Oracle marks needing to be exorcised of dark energies/forces when prevalent i.e., noticed through not sleeping well, feeling haunted, or energy being sucked out of you. Beware of people that cling to you and become like a parasite, just as you should not be a parasite to anyone. Being sucked dry is noticed by how much you're losing due to relationship/business; not just money

but also one's peace of mind, tranquility, or space. In this oracle, one's family or mate's family can be your worst enemy or the biggest asset depending on how much they care about you or love you. Oracle of hurting or injuring the one we love through our actions or not noticing that one is doing this. Beware of being head-strung and willful as in my way or the highway. One must be flexible or understand when one has encountered inflexible individuals that don't contribute to positive things but get in the way and disrupt one's happiness. Beware of justice situations through being involved with people that are into illegal activities. Beware of becoming involved in illegal activities due to not acquiring a career in time. Oracle of never being envious of others, oracle of knowing who's on your side, and not damaging relationships.

HEXAGRAM

42

42 Increase

This is a time of pushing forward and taking advantage of positive energies going your way. It's not that you are going to make a dangerously risky move. But it is time to chance it on something knowing you won't lose. There is an opportunity that can prove profitable or advantageous. Increase is to uplift yourself and others making the best use of a favorable time, that's here. To increase is to also implement or execute thoughts, ideas, or changes that can lead to an improvement wherever it is needed. Make sure that whatever it is that's being forward is tangible and accomplishable. This oracle mentions that good things are on the rise because the correct decisions or choices from the past have positioned you this way. Being organized and having waited is now paying off. It is the right time, and you are in the correct position to advance. The only misfortunes can be attributed to negative behavior, or bad character that will contribute to a shorten increase experience.

Internal Hexagram

23 Splitting Apart

This is an oracle of separations, breakups, and things falling apart. Negative situations have taken hold because of someone overlooked or did not notice what has been brewing underneath. This sign says that one should remain calm and allow for situations to take its course because it's too late to prevent it. The worst indication of this sign is to have thing taken away, removed, or a negative unexpected event transpire. If something has not happened yet, then there might still be time to prevent or sidestep. But this all depends on observing where and how one has been distracted, careless, or unnoticed of your environment.

0
0
0
1

I Ching tetragram 15 - Failure; Yoruba Cowrie 01 - Okana; Yoruba IFa Okana

Okana is to be roped, bound, or tied. Speaks of letting go of things that keep an individually bounded. Also, means needing to bind or secure something so as not to lose it. It all depends on the situation and where the communication is leading too. Never do things without the consent of the divinities. Okana specifically speaks of all types of addictions; sexual, substance, chemical, or shopping i.e., all things destructive to individuals. Oracle of good habits that need to be acquired and bad habits that need to be let go. Okana is an oracle of drought; in essence, if you over-consume or indulge, you'll be left without. Speaks of only remembering God and divinities in times of necessities, or to suit their purpose. Then, when not obtaining what they want, don't believe that spirituality exists or works. Speaks of being dumb, not wanting to learn, or being stubborn. This oracle prescribes becoming educated for the sheer sake of becoming a more intellectual person or remain dumb for the rest of your life. People that can't think for themselves will have to rely on the intelligence of others and for this, they will have to pay. People that forsake education

will have to rely on being lucky and God always compensates those with luck that need it for the lack of wisdom in obtaining things through means that don't require intelligence. But this attitude can lead a person down a path of criminology i.e., anti-social behavior, or dependence on others. Oracle of trickery, fooling, and double standards. The danger in this sign is to have a get-over mentality and not care about who they hurt to obtain their means. Speaks of being mindful, the need for being more understanding, and opened minded. Okana is an oracle of atmospheric changes or going out in bad weather. It is one of wrong timing and doing things at whim without proper planning. Always count on others to do the planning, scheduling, or troubleshooting when unable to do it for yourself. Never say you can do or try to do what you know you don't know how too. On the flip side, people that want to act like they know it all and don't, need to be left dumb.

HEXAGRAM

43

43 Resoluteness Breakthrough

This is the moment of seeing things through, resolving, or catching a break. Speaks of overcoming negative people, situations, or those that wish to keep one down. This oracle teaches to never try to resolve situations using force, when possible, but to win through small progressive advancement that might not be noticed by the enemies or obstructionist. Being aware of dangers and resisting the temptation of meeting it heads on. It is never a sign of weakness to ask for support or seek allies. This oracle's advice to never exhaust yourself trying too hard to overcome something. Negatives have a tendency of weakening and they're lies the opportunity to advance. Patience is necessary for breakthrough because all it takes is the right moment.

01 - The Creative (Heaven, Sky)

Heaven is creation and existence. Without the heavens/space, there wouldn't be a canvas for stars, solar systems, or other universes to have been formed. The creative is the embodiment of Tao (the way) forever moving and creating; the will of God (universal life force). It is now and forever ceaseless, tireless, and moving forward endless and generative. The creative heaven is an oracle of possibilities; beginning with knowing and acknowledging that we are and have been a possibility. Think of the probability of our existence, think of the supernatural occurrence of this solar system manifesting Earth. Let Earth be the divine proof of all things seen and unseen that can be made possible. In essence, if we are possible (life on earth humans etc.) that everything else that you might not believe in is possible. The creative emphasizes you being here and now forever moving forward adapting, failing, and correcting yourself. This can be extended to acknowledging our journey from life to death and back to life. This is the profound oracle of the I Ching that pronounces the existence of the universal life force which was not denied (Tao or will of God) and that's the way it is. For those that accept it wonderful, for those that do not, it is not in their time to do so. In essence, they are not there yet. Ask yourself? Are you there yet? Because this sign expresses that no matter how far you've come, and how far you think you are to go, there is always more. Hence, don't try so hard to tire yourself, but

allow yourself to get there, especially if it is right. This is an oracle were pushing forward and staying on the path leads to success. Hence, to persevere, perseverance takes you further. Oracle of creativity and the strength to move forward in spite of adversities. Although, it's always best to move in the direction of least resistance. Also, moving forward staying on path means, that the shortest distance between two points is to stay on a straight path. To know your direction and not deviate nor zigzag, because indecisions will slow you down and be a waste of time. This oracle prescribes being In harmony with heaven i.e. spirituality, religious inclinations, or practices. To act correctly and in moderation. To move carefully and be aware of dangers and surroundings. Honor, respect, and integrity are keen to succeed; be generous, kind, look to improve yourself, and influence others in positive ways. One must remain loyal and never betray those that support and serve you. To remain humble, let go of ego, pride, and prejudices. To know how to begin things and carry plans, ideas, and aspirations through too fruition. This oracle recommends not being arrogant; never boasting, bragging, or thinking yourself better than others. Not to harm or do evil to anyone. Never take advantage of others or those deemed weaker. But, to prove one's worth in being a symbol of hope, mutual respect of others, supporting those in their walks of life to find their purpose. But most of all, you find your purpose and reason for being. In this way, others and you can achieve happiness in knowing that your life has meant something.

1
1
1
1

I Ching tetragram 01 - Voyage; Yoruba Cowrie 08 - Eyeunle;
Yoruba IFa Ogbe

Ogbe is the oracle of consciousness and will. So, you think
so you are, where your mind takes you, so there will you be. From
a positive point of view, it's where one becomes proud of one's
achievements or how far one has come/traveled. It's to be on
track with achieving goals and to see things through. On a
negative thought, once you've felt that you've reached the top,
then the worst that can happen is to suffer a fall or loss. This is an
oracle of going through separations and adaptation to change;
especially after making decisions that take you in the wrong
direction. It advises not to lose your head i.e., give in to negative
ego, or impulses. It recommends patience and protective actions.
If your time is up where you are, then it's time to move on; life is
not just one journey, but a long road that never ends. Speaking in
this oracle are all situations dealing with the mind, thoughts,
knowledge, understanding, wisdom, and ignorance. Not thinking
properly will lead to confrontations, and one must beware of
never overstepping boundaries. Support unity, but if needing to
separate do so without violence. Know that all endings lead to

new beginnings. Beware of actions that can turn into a justice situation, or lawsuit. But most of all to be organized or bringing order to your life. This is an oracle of being saved by taking a leap of faith and entering some form of spiritual practice. Ogbe is also, road, path, and to be elevated to a new position. There is a tendency towards being or becoming narcissistic, selfish, and not empathic to others, i.e., arrogance and ignorance can lead to this. In essence, not to see through the eyes of others, or feel their concerns. It's not all about you, you affect others, and others you. Having bad behavior is imposing one's will to the extreme of not caring who they step on or who they injure along the way. It's there way or the highway; consequences to actions is sometimes overlooked when it comes to obtaining their means. One must be careful to bite more than one can chew. Things done by force will be met with contention and conflicts will follow. This is a mighty oracle announces blessings and successes that are to be achieved in ones' life. But, only through intelligence, wisdom, patience, and honorable means. All that can be supported by the will of God, and positive divinities in the right way.

HEXAGRAM

44

44 - Coming to Meet, Coupling, Meeting

People meet to discuss, brainstorm, or deliver a message. This can be a friendly hang out, business meeting, seductive meetup/getting to know each other, sexual encounters, or dangerous hidden agenda. This sign focuses on knowing that there is or will be a meeting of some sort. That you are to be or keep in control relative to the kind of meeting this is and never allow for any situation to become negative or dangerous. To always be aware of person's behaviors, attitudes, and intentions. This recommends preparation for the meeting and thinking of all possible outcomes to the meeting, so there are no surprises. Know that all persons gathering are aligned with each other's motives for the meeting. If it is contractual or in competition look to leverage i.e., to be at an advantage point. If it's a one to one, think of the possibility of what they are trying to accomplish and how? Beware of false illusions or talking a good game for the sake of persuasion. Always be mindful, or conscientious of who's influencing who.

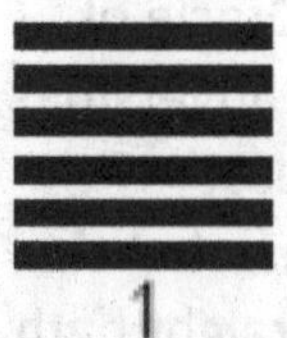

1

01 - The Creative (Heaven, Sky)

Heaven is creation and existence. Without the heavens/space, there wouldn't be a canvas for stars, solar systems, or other universes to have been formed. The creative is the embodiment of Tao (the way) forever moving and creating; the will of God (universal life force). It is now and forever ceaseless, tireless, and moving forward endless and generative. The creative heaven is an oracle of possibilities; beginning with knowing and acknowledging that we are and have been a possibility. Think of the probability of our existence, think of the supernatural occurrence of this solar system manifesting Earth. Let Earth be the divine proof of all things seen and unseen that can be made possible. In essence, if we are possible (life on earth humans etc.) that everything else that you might not believe in is possible. The creative emphasizes you being here and now forever moving forward adapting, failing, and correcting yourself. This can be extended to acknowledging our journey from life to death and back to life. This is the profound oracle of the I Ching that pronounces the existence of the universal life force which was not denied (Tao or will of God) and that's the way it is. For those that accept it wonderful, for those that do not, it is not in their time to do so. In essence, they are not there yet. Ask yourself? Are you there yet? Because this sign expresses that no matter how far you've come, and how far you think you are to go, there is always more. Hence, don't try so hard to tire yourself, but

allow yourself to get there, especially if it is right. This is an oracle were pushing forward and staying on the path leads to success. Hence, to persevere, perseverance takes you further. Oracle of creativity and the strength to move forward in spite of adversities. Although, it's always best to move in the direction of least resistance. Also, moving forward staying on path means, that the shortest distance between two points is to stay on a straight path. To know your direction and not deviate nor zigzag, because indecisions will slow you down and be a waste of time. This oracle prescribes being In harmony with heaven i.e. spirituality, religious inclinations, or practices. To act correctly and in moderation. To move carefully and be aware of dangers and surroundings. Honor, respect, and integrity are keen to succeed; be generous, kind, look to improve yourself, and influence others in positive ways. One must remain loyal and never betray those that support and serve you. To remain humble, let go of ego, pride, and prejudices. To know how to begin things and carry plans, ideas, and aspirations through too fruition. This oracle recommends not being arrogant; never boasting, bragging, or thinking yourself better than others. Not to harm or do evil to anyone. Never take advantage of others or those deemed weaker. But, to prove one's worth in being a symbol of hope, mutual respect of others, supporting those in their walks of life to find their purpose. But most of all, you find your purpose and reason for being. In this way, others and you can achieve happiness in knowing that your life has meant something.

Internal Tetragram Geomancy Code

1
1
1
0

I Ching tetragram 02 - Corruption; Yoruba Cowrie 03 - Ogunda;
Yoruba IFa Ogunda

      This is an oracle of being dedicated to a profession, as well
as safeguarding your position, title, work, or livelihood. It's to
avoid putting your freedom at risk i.e., justice situation. Avoid
putting your life at risk through physical altercations, or
quarreling. It's an oracle of fights, violence, stealing, or desiring a
big score; in essence, beware of desiring to obtain things through
force or illegal means. Never take advantage of the weak, mistreat
others, or you'll suffer being mistreated. Someone needs
protection against justice situations or help in winning a court
case, or battle in general. Beware of injury working with tools,
vehicles, accidents due to stress or over working. Oracle of having
strength but knowing when and how to use it. Wasted strength
depletes and turns into a weakness. One needs to be tenderer
and earn the respect of mates and others through kindness.
Ogunda teaches us that war is necessary for peace to reign in the
end. But everything doesn't have to be a battle when you can win
with wisdom. The greatest asset of Ogunda is to become
educated, acquiring skills, or recognizing one's talent and profiting

from it. This is an oracle of creating, inventing, constructing, building, and engineering. Learn, especially about what tools you will need that can support your talents or make your life easier. Oracle of work, and making oneself useful, not useless.

HEXAGRAM

45

45 Gathering Together

A reason to gather is coming planned or unplanned. When gathering is to promote a positive venture with like minds meet and share the same goals and objects good things transpire. When a gathering is not productive, it becomes a waste of time. Large gatherings need to be planned and good people need to be protected from those with bad intent or a negative agenda. A medium gathering can be planned, and all members know what they are to contribute to the gathering. When it is a small gathering, this can be for the planning and determination of what is to be expected by individuals, groups, or people. Nevertheless, a leader is necessary that everyone can respect and listen to. If not a leader, then a mediator that supports the overcoming of conflicts. Because when people gather there will always be those for or against something or other, and everyone needs to be prepared for it.

Internal Hexagram

53

53 Gradual Development

All things that develop in time brings success. This is contingent upon acting correcting and staying on path and true to the cause till the end. All things that start off to quickly can reach a certain level, and then decline. Measures must be taken along the way to avoid the decline. Consideration must be given to the possibilities of things that can go wrong. When is someone not sincere or clear in their objective and fool others into meeting their selfish needs? This sign is one that prophecies the establishment of a relations, good relationships, or finding the right relationship. The relationship is proven to be successful if it leads to a good pairing. Both individuals or parties have found they match in goals and aspirations. Then with the correct temperance, motivation, and patience dedication and discipline will bring success. Gradual development ultimately implies sacrifice, effort, and consistency – solutions are not overnight. Also, one must be mindful of how to fix things along the way, in the event of mistakes and things going wrong.

1
0
0
0

I Ching tetragram 08 - Authority; Yoruba Cowrie 06 - Obara;
Yoruba IFa Obara

Obara says, "There can't be changed without revolution - chaos or torment." An oracle of wisdom, intelligence, and learning how to better live or coexist with those in your environment. Business related relative to marketing and knowing how to deliver goods to markets. The market rises, and the markets fall. It's where wheels turn/move forward, but there are times when we need to turn back or go backwards. Obara is an oracle where being proud leads to starvation, being left alone, or being put to the side. Oracle of success or failure, where the tongue, verb, or speaking can save you or do you in. The tongue can be used for evil, as it can be used for good. Good when it's used to praise, pray for good things, and bless. Evil went it's used to offend, false witness, and lie. So, mind your tongue. Speaks of knowing how to stay standing up and not falling after having worked hard in obtaining a position or move up in life. Speaks of good business relations when fair. Speaks of difficulties in maintaining relationships (personal, social) due to being difficult to satisfy. In Obara one needs to maintain focus on education and utilizing

one's talents or gifts to become successful. One is not to allow matters of the heart, emotions, or promiscuity to get in the way of one's success. Concentration and focus on achievements will bring happiness and many positive things. Giving in to pettiness, childishness, egotism, and distractions will lead to failure. The individual from a young age must learn to discern lies, and not fall into anti-social behavior. This will inevitably lead to doom. This is an oracle of planning, setting goals, and knowing how to execute the plan. Oracle of conquering and escaping danger when knowing how not to be in the wrong place, and at the wrong time. This is an oracle of not being a liar, learning that there is no honor in lying.

HEXAGRAM

46

46 Pushing Upwards Ascending

A time has come to push upward or ascend. There is always effort involved to pushing upward, and it is time for your efforts to be rewarded. There is help or support at this time, hence don't be shy to approach the ones that can. When coming across resistance in pushing upward, one should not be inflexible. Even an obtainable small gain is proof of advancing. But don't be surprised if the gain is greater than expected because the timing is right. Always show appreciation when receiving support or being allowed to ascend. This sends a message that you are not being arrogant, taking your blessing for granted, and you're giving merit to others; a very good sign of being humble.

Internal Hexagram

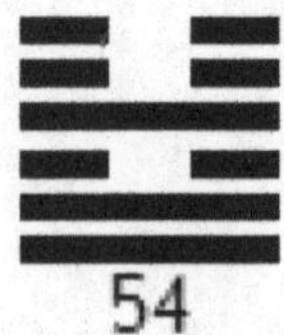

54

54 Marrying Maiden

Wishing to marry, or for a binding relationship as we both shall live, till death do we part. This requires aside from love and respect; communication with comprehension, patience with tolerance, and final asking each other if you still want to make this work. Granted ego, selfishness, pride, and insincerity must be tossed out the window. Marriage is about being all for one and one for all with the mutual goal of forging a legacy. If you are too young or too immature you are not ready and you will fail. If you are marrying for convenience, settling, or premeditated intent you'll pay in the long run, and it will fail too. Let's say the marriage is business oriented such is a partnership. But, even for this to be successful, not only should this partnership be for the same reason, but both must put in the work equally and balanced. One needs to offset the other, work as a team. In essence, recognize each other's strength and weaknesses, and both diligently work at improving them with each other supporting the other. Never forget to seek advice and counsel from those equipped with the knowledge to mediate conflicts all for the sake of the marriage remaining true.

0
1
1
0

I Ching tetragram 10 - Agreements; Yoruba Cowrie 15 - Marunla; Yoruba IFa Iwori

Iwori is the oracle of your head's view on things or your head getting around to the right thought processes. It is to know what it means to think; think goodness as much as to know what it is to think evil and be evil. Oracle of never thinking one is a know it all, or to believe they know more than God, his divinities, and the land of the dead. It's the oracle of scientific discovery, technology, psychology, and all-around wisdom. Yet, maintaining a level head being constructive and not destructive. Beware of a mental breakdown due to overexerting one's brain in trying too hard to accomplish desires. It is wisdom to know that what is meant for you comes with little effort. Because it is meant be and easy, it is right and the right timing too. What is not meant is known because of the struggle that it takes trying to obtain it, only to lose it because it was not meant to be. The individual must beware of becoming overbearing, autocratic, or tyrannical because one will end up alone. Where privileged individuals can lose everything being overconfident, and making willful mistakes, they need to listen to others too and respect their advice or

opinion. The greatest challenge is to learn how to obtain things by the grace of God, and divinities, not thinking all things come just because of your efforts. This demands great patience and allowing the divinities to bring things to you. Iwori's inner or external battle relates to finding their right place in the world. Frustration can come from the inability to uphold a position in society that is recognizable. They have a great need to feel that they are not just contributing to family, community, or society but also leaving a mark. Iwori is an oracle where families destroy one another through infighting, competing, and showing who's the dominate one. Yet, they as a unit become a force to be reckoned with when united or focus on the greater good of the whole family. Individuals should work on forging a legacy that lasts generations in this way they will truly make their mark on life.

HEXAGRAM

47

47 Oppression, Entangled, Imprisoned

Choked is what comes to mind, being held back, and bound. This is a hard time because one has no control. One's mind is consumed with thinking on how to get out being oppressed or feeling imprisoned. Begin with analyzing the events that has led to this condition and look for others in a position to assist. One needs to remain in good character, and positive behavior. Clear and opened mindedness is an asset. Do not allow the situations or this period to weaken you spirit of resolve. Turn your oppression into a test of your will to succeed despite any hardship. Don't give in to depression, turn this into waiting it out. All things pass but if you give in to a mental breakdown because of what problem you know this is, you'll not see the light at the end of the tunnel. Know that punishing oneself, pointing fingers, and blaming does nothing. But acknowledging and being realistic of what's transpiring can lead to figuring a way out or escape.

37

37 Family or Group

Blood is thicker than water, and everyone in a family carry mutual traits. Hence, in a family folks must strive towards getting along. Getting along with your family is like getting along with oneself. This is attributed to all members recognizing each other's roles and position; know yourself and what you can contribute to the whole. This begins with a good leader that can motivate and inspire others as well as keep the family organized and intact. All members must maintain good character in meeting individual goals. The family or group is a collective. This means that all have separate responsibilities, but when putting them all together working in common interest, they accomplish optimum goals. Recognition must be given especially to those that have or share in the task of keeping everyone together. In relation to an actual family, one should ask if one believes in family, and if you do, will it require a marriage. Always remember that when forging a family, it becomes something greater than oneself. A family is a legacy, so nothing should be thought of in short term. Legacies are meant to exist long past our existence and withstand the test of generations.

1
0
1
0

I Ching tetragram 06 - Dissolution; Yoruba Cowrie 05 - Oche; Yoruba IFa Oche

Oracle of the blood being thicker than water, blood being the transporter of cells for living organisms to function. In essence, blood is life. Oracle where money came into the world, and today is the lifeblood of society, business, commerce, or government economies. This is an oracle of fights over money, and in some cases over livelihood (bringing food to your table). Oracle of being cheated or feeling cheated. It's the oracle where the money is cursed, or "the root to all evil." Human blood feeds money i.e., the blood sweat, and tears of those that work to survive. Rich folks curse it because many of them don't want to lose it. Poor folks curse it because they don't have it, and it eludes them. In Oche negativity stems from the decomposition of things, corruption, failures, when situations fall apart. Uncleanliness, impurities, or filthiness corrupts and generates diseases. Hence, sanitize, wash, purify, and never allow germs, parasites, or viruses to take hold. Taking care of one's digestion, and blood is important to avoid illnesses or diseases from an early age. Oche is an oracle of dysfunctional, disorganized family, relationships, or

affairs. The protection of the family, economic position, and not allowing for relationship problems getting in the way of happiness is key to being successful. In this oracle one is to make one's spirituality stronger through dedication, devotion, and being responsible with one's gift; otherwise, one loses the gift and gives way to the decomposition of all things. Oche is an oracle of protecting that which you've worked so hard to maintain. Love God and his divinities so you attend them, so will they support you in getting out of situations and resolving for better living. Oche is an oracle of needing to be saved through taking a leap of faith and entering a shamanistic priestly way of life.

HEXAGRAM

48

48 - The Well

Think of all the things that a well can represent. A place for drawing water for quenching thirst, for cooking, washing, healing, and a place to gather. A Well is a place to draw energy from for sustaining ourselves and community. From a well a village can be born, that turns into a town, and a town into a city. A well makes it possible for people to gather, live, work, and prosper. This oracle teaches that we need to have a source from where we can draw energy, knowledge, spirituality, economic well-being, and love. We cannot allow our well to dry or our sustenance and the many uses that our well serves will also cease to be of use. How do we keep enthusiastic, optimistic, creative, and passionate for ourselves and contribute to others? We need to continually assess and measure the levels in all these things and fix, upgrade, or replace old parts of the well, or renew it somewhere else if it starts to go dry. But we must always have a place from where we can draw sustenance from.

38

38 Opposition

When opposition arrives, one needs to be diligent and advance slowly, not rush, nor push forward spontaneously. This is a time where someone, or something does not blend, mix, unite, and goes against others. Know that when people oppose one another problems will arise. Hence, meeting each other halfway in small matters can lead to better things or problem solving. Look at the benefits of resolving a little bit at a time and make changes that can bring about a positive outcome, even when there is opposition. Finger pointing, arguments, and stubbornness won't solve anything. Coming to terms due to mutual respect and using diplomacy will set things back on track and all will benefit.

0
1
1
0

I Ching tetragram 10 - Agreements; Yoruba Cowrie 15 - Marunla;
Yoruba IFa Iwori

Iwori is the oracle of your head's view on things or your
head getting around to the right thought processes. It is to know
what it means to think; think goodness as much as to know what
it is to think evil and be evil. Oracle of never thinking one is a
know it all, or to believe they know more than God, his divinities,
and the land of the dead. It's the oracle of scientific discovery,
technology, psychology, and all-around wisdom. Yet, maintaining
a level head being constructive and not destructive. Beware of a
mental breakdown due to overexerting one's brain in trying too
hard to accomplish desires. It is wisdom to know that what is
meant for you comes with little effort. Because it is meant be and
easy, it is right and the right timing too. What is not meant is
known because of the struggle that it takes trying to obtain it,
only to lose it because it was not meant to be. The individual must
beware of becoming overbearing, autocratic, or tyrannical
because one will end up alone. Where privileged individuals can
lose everything being overconfident, and making willful mistakes,
they need to listen to others too and respect their advice or

opinion. The greatest challenge is to learn how to obtain things by the grace of God, and divinities, not thinking all things come just because of your efforts. This demands great patience and allowing the divinities to bring things to you. Iwori's inner or external battle relates to finding their right place in the world. Frustration can come from the inability to uphold a position in society that is recognizable. They have a great need to feel that they are not just contributing to family, community, or society but also leaving a mark. Iwori is an oracle where families destroy one another through infighting, competing, and showing who's the dominate one. Yet, they as a unit become a force to be reckoned with when united or focus on the greater good of the whole family. Individuals should work on forging a legacy that lasts generations in this way they will truly make their mark on life.

HEXAGRAM

49

49 Revolution Rebelliousness

     When an individual or people are mistreated, oppressed, and abused they will rebel. A rebellion can be done controlled, with intelligence, and nonviolently or disorganized and out of control, and end in violence. When a revolution is imminent because someone can't take it anymore, and an abuse has gone too far. It is most beneficial to both parties that it be conducted non-aggressively, and the oppressing party concede defeat from those that desire change. The best way for change to occur is to have the many supporters or allies on your side. This will make it difficult for any oppressors to deny or ignore the need for change. It is important to keep in mind the timing to rebel and place. Because the conditions must be favorable and conducive to the transition being accepted but also not counter attacked. Foresight in knowing the particulars on how a revolution can fail, or how long it can last is important. Safeguards or measures must be in place to secure a win, or things will revert to the old ways. Unless the reason for rebelling was completely wrong to begin with.

44

44 - Coming to Meet, Coupling, Meeting

People meet to discuss, brainstorm, or deliver a message. This can be a friendly hang out, business meeting, seductive meetup/getting to know each other, sexual encounters, or dangerous hidden agenda. This sign focuses on knowing that there is or will be a meeting of some sort. That you are to be or keep in control relative to the kind of meeting this is and never allow for any situation to become negative or dangerous. To always be aware of person's behaviors, attitudes, and intentions. This recommends preparation for the meeting and thinking of all possible outcomes to the meeting, so there are no surprises. Know that all persons gathering are aligned with each other's motives for the meeting. If it is contractual or in competition look to leverage i.e., to be at an advantage point. If it's a one to one, think of the possibility of what they are trying to accomplish and how? Beware of false illusions or talking a good game for the sake of persuasion. Always be mindful, or conscientious of who's influencing who.

1
1
0
1

I Ching tetragram 03 - Activities; Yoruba Cowrie 13 - Metanla; Yoruba IFa Irete

Irete is an oracle of being sought after looked for or found. Beware of investigations, or being probed, and getting caught. Irete represents escaping, an escape, climbing out of a hole/ditch, or getting out of a rut. When desperate or in despair there will be someone or a situation will arise that will give way to the needed support in overcoming the difficulty. Irete is an oracle of upward mobility as in stepping up a ladder or striving towards bettering oneself, rising above the rest, or rising to the occasion. It is one of undergoing physical challenges, beware of early disease or injuries to one's limbs via falling and fracturing. Also beware of accidents, not being mindful. When it comes to women this is a sign that relates to difficult pregnancies. In general, beware of love triangles and promiscuity, which can lead to STDs. Learning how to attend to spirit guides and ancestors is important because it's a sign that marks communications with them. Learn to be obedient and listen to ancestral advice. There will be a reunion or gathering soon. The person needs much love, romanticism, and finding the correct mate to ensure happiness. This is not

something that happens trying too hard. It's something the happens being at the right place and right time. In Irete religious activities are much more favorable to the person's energy than social ones (partying).

HEXAGRAM

50

The Caldron Stewing Brewing

     Cooking, brewing, stewing, making, creating, and experimenting. All these things require effort, time, and patience. Think also of what goes into making something taste just right, and others approve of it. There will be moments when our ingredients in the pot or recipes doesn't come out right. But we don't give up we try again make adjustments using other ingredients or difference procedure, and it works. This implies dedication and devotion to a vocation because one enjoys it. Without passion or putting passion into our work things won't taste right. Things done with pleasure and with good will is satisfying to all persons involved. This oracle does not just imply making something good happen, but to continually rise to an occasion. The result is the approval of something well done. If not, you'll have to go back to the drawing board.

43

43 Resoluteness Breakthrough

This is the moment of seeing things through, resolving, or catching a break. Speaks of overcoming negative people, situations, or those that wish to keep one down. This oracle teaches to never try to resolve situations using force, when possible, but to win through small progressive advancement that might not be noticed by the enemies or obstructionist. Being aware of dangers and resisting the temptation of meeting it heads on. It is never a sign of weakness to ask for support or seek allies. This oracle's advice to never exhaust yourself trying too hard to overcome something. Negatives have a tendency of weakening and they're lies the opportunity to advance. Patience is necessary for breakthrough because all it takes is the right moment.

Internal Tetragram Geomancy Code

1
1
1
0

I Ching tetragram 02 - Corruption; Yoruba Cowrie 03 - Ogunda;
Yoruba IFa Ogunda

This is an oracle of being dedicated to a profession, as well
as safeguarding your position, title, work, or livelihood. It's to
avoid putting your freedom at risk i.e., justice situation. Avoid
putting your life at risk through physical altercations, or
quarreling. It's an oracle of fights, violence, stealing, or desiring a
big score; in essence, beware of desiring to obtain things through
force or illegal means. Never take advantage of the weak, mistreat
others, or you'll suffer being mistreated. Someone needs
protection against justice situations or help in winning a court
case, or battle in general. Beware of injury working with tools,
vehicles, accidents due to stress or over working. Oracle of having
strength but knowing when and how to use it. Wasted strength
depletes and turns into a weakness. One needs to be tenderer
and earn the respect of mates and others through kindness.
Ogunda teaches us that war is necessary for peace to reign in the
end. But everything doesn't have to be a battle when you can win
with wisdom. The greatest asset of Ogunda is to become
educated, acquiring skills, or recognizing one's talent and profiting

from it. This is an oracle of creating, inventing, constructing, building, and engineering. Learn, especially about what tools you will need that can support your talents or make your life easier. Oracle of work, and making oneself useful, not useless.

HEXAGRAM

51 Thunder Shock Movement

Shock is good when it's used to awaken something dormant, too slow, or about to give out. Think of shocking the heart, being shocked into realizing or acknowledging something. Even being horrified by someone's actions, and unforeseen incident, or tragedy. Shock can be arousing and stimulating when it's joyful, ticklish, and in good taste. But, also deadly like a bolt of lightning when sudden and unaware. Striking shock or fear in someone can be necessary at times; but one must be careful not to cause retaliation in defense of your actions. When an individual's shock others and never prepared them for it, they can be alienated or suffer separation from those not appreciating the shock. For these types of surprises there needs to not just be reason, but it must be supported with proof, evidence, or support of others. In this way, everyone will know that the shock was necessary. Shock implies electricity that's always moving, a bolt of energy, hence get moving.

39

39 Obstruction Hesitation

To be obstructed is to be blocked, held back, or not allowed to move forward. There are moments that this is due to the environment or timing. Time meaning year, month, day, season, or moment. There are positive seasons and negative ones. We can't always have things our way. Identify where the obstruction is coming from and formulate a plan for getting out of the way of what is blocking or understand that it can unblock itself. There are times in which we need the advice of someone wiser that can help us see how to remove the obstruction. Then, there are times where we need to hesitate or obstruct things for ourselves to avoid a foreseen danger. Hence, stop evaluate whether some situation was a bad choice, or mistake that is being caught on time. All deliberate hesitation or holding back will conclude with the correct decision as too when to move forward again. Hopefully, by then one has a better plan to execute.

1
0
0
1

I Ching tetragram 07 - Obstacles; Yoruba Cowrie 07 - Odi; Yoruba IFa Odi

Odi is an oracle of great luck, and of having strong spirit guides, and ancestor links that when used properly and developed will bring about great things to a person's life. Oracle of individuals that can be a bit obnoxious overbearing or surrounded by obnoxious overbearing people and situations. The greatest downfall in the person's life according to this oracle is gossip, being nosy, and false witnessing. Also, speaking out of context, or giving out information to the wrong individuals at the wrong time. It's an oracle of having some sort of habit or addiction, i.e., an addictive personality. Substances abuse situations will lead to the destruction not only of the person's organism but of others and all happiness around them. Speaks of the creation of the marketplace learning sales, money management, having own business, or running someone's business. Oracle of feminism, and the gift of being a woman in bringing forth life into the world. The individual must be more objective, toughen their heart, and control emotions. Because this oracle is of being emotional, or emotional situations being hard for the person to handle. Keeping

a marriage will be a challenge and difficult due to emotional imbalances, jealousy issues, pride, ego, or constantly picking the wrong individual. Speaks of suffering childhood traumas that still affect the individual even throughout adulthood. Getting along with one's family can be difficult. Oracle where family members become enemies of one another. Ancestors demand family unity. Avoid indecisiveness, selfishness, and promiscuity. Oracle of a hole, crater, ditch, crevasse, or grave. Advice is to not make decisions or make lifestyle choices that lead to an early grave, for many pitfalls.

HEXAGRAM

52

52 The Mountain Keeping Still

Majestic, breath taking, imposing, and a landmark is a mountain. It represents unmovable stillness, something powerful and difficult to traverse/pass. The first thing one does when one sees a Mountain is stop and be taken by its grandeur. When facing a monumental situation, this oracle tells us to hold back, keep still, stop, and analyze how one is to move forward. One must recognize that obstacles time is need for research, brainstorming, and planning before execution. Will one go over the mountain, around it, or through it. The oracle always implies rest, to be at peace, or find peace from a positive perspective. It implies waiting, not moving forward in the face of danger, and trying to cross a difficult path without knowing all particulars of what lays ahead. Keeping still is advantageous when one can release tension and clear one's mind to plan on how to move. Imagine being on a mountain listening to the sounds of this forest, taking in the silence. This is a time for seclusion, going into meditation, or seeking self-care. Take your time.

40 Deliverance Release

Anytime one releases tension, stress, or is released from being enslaved/imprisoned is a good thing. This is to be delivered, may we be delivered from or out of all negative situations and intent. Have deliverance is to be liberated, untangled, and unbound. There are bindings that are unnecessary, unneeded, and difficult to get out of. Recognize when you are putting yourself into an unpleasant situation binding to something that doesn't provide a blessing. This is an oracle of having a good outcome relative to being set free. It points to having been or being disturbed bothered, or unwillingly attached, even by mistake. There is nothing better than freedom. Hence, if you need to let someone go do so, for everyone's happiness. Selfishness, and control for the sake of egotism and stubbornness will never bring success in the end. They're many things that we must let go or let be free.

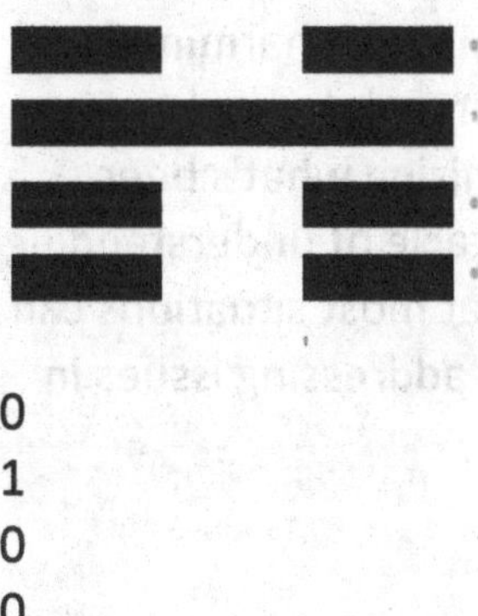

0
1
0
0

I Ching tetragram 12 - Violation; Yoruba Cowrie 14 - Merinla;
Yoruba IFa Ika

     Ika means to know how to get around situations. It is an
oracle of finding the correct approach to things. One needs to find
themselves, and their correct way of being. But most importantly
stability in life, i.e., where or what brings stability. If the individual
has been kicked out, lost their job/home, their stability? They will
need to help in getting back on track. Look to spirituality for this
support or find those that can give guidance and ritual work to
bring you back from the loss. Ika is an oracle of going to battle, or
having to battle, along with the work that is needed to win. It's
where we as young folks hit the road of life in a direction towards
finding our profession, place, position, where one is going to be
successful. If you find yourself struggling to much and going
through obstacles and hard times. This is a definite indicator that
you are not where you need to be. Ika is an oracle of avoiding
battles or getting out them. Avoid spiritual battles with folks that
utilize spirituality to do harm. Suggest too, allow elders or more
experienced people to help you through guidance; don't try to be
a know it all. Ika is an oracle of helping others and through

goodwill unto others, returning favors or someone least expected help you when most needed occurs. Hence, one is not to reject help due to pride. This is an oracle of the family not harming one another. Beware of being kicked out your home, job, work, relationship, or someplace due to not recognizing what's been going on. In essence you snooze you lose. Oracle of understanding what is evident or inevitable. Understand that most situations can be resolved just by getting out of the way or addressing issues in time.

HEXAGRAM

53

53 Gradual Development

All things that develop in time brings success. This is contingent upon acting correcting and staying on path and true to the cause till the end. All things that start off to quickly can reach a certain level, and then decline. Measures must be taken along the way to avoid the decline. Consideration must be given to the possibilities of things that can go wrong. When is someone not sincere or clear in their objective and fool others into meeting their selfish needs? This sign is one that prophecies the establishment of a relations, good relationships, or finding the right relationship. The relationship is proven to be successful if it leads to a good pairing. Both individuals or parties have found they match in goals and aspirations. Then with the correct temperance, motivation, and patience dedication and discipline will bring success. Gradual development ultimately implies sacrifice, effort, and consistency – solutions are not overnight. Also, one must be mindful of how to fix things along the way, in the event of mistakes and things going wrong.

56

56 The Wanderer, Traveler, or Traveling

A traveler, traveling, wanderer, explorer, or exploring. For this, one must have good manners be polite, empathetic, respectful, conscientious, and opened minded. How can one explore without an opened mind? Think of being stubborn, set-in one's ways, or with prejudices, and meet someone of another culture, tradition, or race. They will not last as a good traveler, if they have no respect. A wanderer can only be accepted by a stranger or strangers when they can accept the ideas, understandings, and knowledge of others without reservations. A wanderer must share, work side by side with people they meet, open heartedly, and share knowledge with others. Wanderers are the first to understand that we all part of a bigger picture in this world. We are not alone and need to contribute as part of a whole. But, most of all we were all made differently because it is necessary, and good that we are. When being humble, hospitable, and helpful to strangers, you are not only accepted but remembered. In essence never burn bridges keep friendships true and you'll be accepted again.

0
1
0
0

I Ching tetragram 12 - Violation; Yoruba Cowrie 14 - Merinla; Yoruba IFa Ika

Ika means to know how to get around situations. It is an oracle of finding the correct approach to things. One needs to find themselves, and their correct way of being. But most importantly stability in life, i.e., where or what brings stability. If the individual has been kicked out, lost their job/home, their stability? They will need to help in getting back on track. Look to spirituality for this support or find those that can give guidance and ritual work to bring you back from the loss. Ika is an oracle of going to battle, or having to battle, along with the work that is needed to win. It's where we as young folks hit the road of life in a direction towards finding our profession, place, position, where one is going to be successful. If you find yourself struggling to much and going through obstacles and hard times. This is a definite indicator that you are not where you need to be. Ika is an oracle of avoiding battles or getting out them. Avoid spiritual battles with folks that utilize spirituality to do harm. Suggest too, allow elders or more experienced people to help you through guidance; don't try to be a know it all. Ika is an oracle of helping others and through

goodwill unto others, returning favors or someone least expected help you when most needed occurs. Hence, one is not to reject help due to pride. This is an oracle of the family not harming one another. Beware of being kicked out your home, job, work, relationship, or someplace due to not recognizing what's been going on. In essence you snooze you lose. Oracle of understanding what is evident or inevitable. Understand that most situations can be resolved just by getting out of the way or addressing issues in time.

HEXAGRAM

54

54 Marrying Maiden

Wishing to marry, or for a binding relationship as we both shall live, till death do we part. This requires aside from love and respect; communication with comprehension, patience with tolerance, and final asking each other if you still want to make this work. Granted ego, selfishness, pride, and insincerity must be tossed out the window. Marriage is about being all for one and one for all with the mutual goal of forging a legacy. If you are too young or too immature you are not ready and you will fail. If you are marrying for convenience, settling, or premeditated intent you'll pay in the long run, and it will fail too. Let's say the marriage is business oriented such is a partnership. But, even for this to be successful, not only should this partnership be for the same reason, but both must put in the work equally and balanced. One needs to offset the other, work as a team. In essence, recognize each other's strength and weaknesses, and both diligently work at improving them with each other supporting the other. Never forget to seek advice and counsel from those equipped with the knowledge to mediate conflicts all for the sake of the marriage remaining true.

63

63 After Completion, Completed

This oracle signifies taking a break after completing tasks, ventures, assignments, or milestone achievement. This is a time to get reorganized for the next plan or strategy that needs execution. The break is for a visualization of the future an outreach mental assessment of what is to follow. Physical labor does not need to be included at this time just the brainstorming that leads to proper organization of ideas. It is also forward thinking for clarity in direction in way things should go and staying ahead. The oracle advises to completely resolve all outstanding issues, so that any new venture can begin on a clean slate. Never carry old baggage to new situations, you will be contaminating it, in essence extending what should have been complete. This defeats the purpose of starting something new.

Internal Tetragram Geomancy Code

1
0
1
1

I Ching tetragram 05 - Grace; Yoruba Cowrie 16 - Meridilogun; Yoruba IFa Otura

Otura speaks of living in an inhospitable place. It's to be surrounded or live among con artists, and thieves. Also, to avoid being conned or tricked, someone is to be outwitted. Never be the first to know or know the most and the last to take advantage of opportunities. This is a sign of not being given recognition for your efforts or taken for granted. Don't take things for granted, life, family, relationship, jobs, or career, etc. Oracle of being too slow to take advantage of an opportunity due to being distracted. The person needs to have a sharp mind and keep things in order. Not saying you are going to do but doing it, especially with honor. The sooner an individual acquires the necessary skills, and identifies their talents or career, the sooner they will be successful. Oracle prescribes not allowing situations to drag. Bringing closure to situations will allow for one to go on to the next thing without skipping a beat. This sign doesn't permit delaying because carelessness and making mistakes will take hold. Oracle of knowing how to live within your means, respect, and worships the forces of God. How well and proficient individual

works with the divine forces, so will their grace bring them blessings. Speaks of dark forces robbing the person's luck, happiness, and economic well-being when not appeased or expunged in time. Yet, Otura is an oracle of resolving with good luck when situations are taken care of in time. Identify grace, gift, or being gracious in doing things with good taste, will win the hearts of others. And, with this comes the necessary support, not being alone, or left alone with all the weight upon your shoulders.

HEXAGRAM

55

55 Abundance

This oracle supports the right to being happy knowing you have abundance. To have in abundance to be abundant means to be able to share with others. It is right to be content and understand the level of conformity that leads to feeling and knowing your abundance. We always should be thankful, especially when there are those that have less. This oracle personifies the idea of where three can eat, so can four because we will make enough to share. Granted one is not to give it all away, because replenishing one's gifts might not be easy. And of course, you would not desire folks to take you for granted or be unappreciative of your generosity. Those that have come to experience abundance are to be good leaders, heads of family, or organization. What good is it to have if not to influence, and support others in a positive way. Abundance is not limited to economics, it also includes love, healing, and spirituality. The key to abundance is maintaining or knowing how to regenerate that which is being depleted through giving. Hence, abundance is to first serve the owner and then what is shared is done so out of kindness and the good will to do good.

28

28 - Preponderance of the Great - Excessiveness or Extra

Oracle of excessiveness, extra, too much to handle, or overindulging. This also means too beware of gluttony, greed, or exaggeration. The advice is to understand when something is too much, overkill, or know when something is being overdone. Something will break when it is in excess, it stresses that all things must be handled correctly and with care for what things to not break. Proper due diligence (homework), evaluations, and executions will give way to successful outcome. Excess, or extra is good when it meets expectations or surpasses them. Preponderance of the great also means to accept change or know that change is unavoidable no matter how much we try to push forward or hold back. The individual might want to but forces more powerful are pushing for things to manifest despite of attempting to control them.

1
1
0
1

I Ching tetragram 03 - Activities; Yoruba Cowrie 13 - Metanla; Yoruba IFa Irete

Irete is an oracle of being sought after looked for or found. Beware of investigations, or being probed, and getting caught. Irete represents escaping, an escape, climbing out of a hole/ditch, or getting out of a rut. When desperate or in despair there will be someone or a situation will arise that will give way to the needed support in overcoming the difficulty. Irete is an oracle of upward mobility as in stepping up a ladder or striving towards bettering oneself, rising above the rest, or rising to the occasion. It is one of undergoing physical challenges, beware of early disease or injuries to one's limbs via falling and fracturing. Also beware of accidents, not being mindful. When it comes to women this is a sign that relates to difficult pregnancies. In general, beware of love triangles and promiscuity, which can lead to STDs. Learning how to attend to spirit guides and ancestors is important because it's a sign that marks communications with them. Learn to be obedient and listen to ancestral advice. There will be a reunion or gathering soon. The person needs much love, romanticism, and finding the correct mate to ensure happiness. This is not

something that happens trying too hard. It's something the
happens being at the right place and right time. In Irete religious
activities are much more favorable to the person's energy than
social ones (partying).

HEXAGRAM

56

56 The Wanderer, Traveler, or Traveling

A traveler, traveling, wanderer, explorer, or exploring. For this, must have good manners be polite, empathetic, respectful, conscientious, and opened minded. How can one explore without an opened mind? Think of being stubborn, set-in one's ways, or with prejudices, and meet someone of another culture, tradition, or race. They will not last as a good traveler, if they have no respect. A wanderer can only be accepted by a stranger or strangers when they can accept the ideas, understandings, and knowledge of others without reservations. A wanderer must share, work side by side with people they meet, open heartedly, and share knowledge with others. Wanderers are the first to understand that we all part of a bigger picture in this world. We are not alone and need to contribute as part of a whole. But, most of all we were all made differently because it is necessary, and good that we are. When being humble, hospitable, and helpful to strangers, you are not only accepted but remembered. In essence never burn bridges keep friendships true and you'll be accepted again.

28 - Preponderance of the Great - Excessiveness or Extra

Oracle of excessiveness, extra, too much to handle, or overindulging. This also means too beware of gluttony, greed, or exaggeration. The advice is to understand when something is too much, overkill, or know when something is being overdone. Something will break when it is in excess, it stresses that all things must be handled correctly and with care for what things to not break. Proper due diligence (homework), evaluations, and executions will give way to successful outcome. Excess, or extra is good when it meets expectations or surpasses them. Preponderance of the great also means to accept change or know that change is unavoidable no matter how much we try to push forward or hold back. The individual might want to but forces more powerful are pushing for things to manifest despite of attempting to control them.

1
1
0
0

I Ching tetragram 03 - Enthusiasm; Yoruba Cowrie 04 - Iroso;
Yoruba IFa Iroso

Iroso means the unknown, mysterious, hidden, secrets, and surprises. This is a sign of riches, obtaining, inheriting, or achieving status. It's to avoid entrapments of being made part of a grander scheme. Iroso has a saying, "No one knows the mysteries that lie beneath the depths of the seas." As in a blessing, which can come out of nowhere; as well as trouble when taken in a negative context. It's an oracle of discovery as much as it is of exposure to danger. It announces a business takeover or being taken advantage of. It recommends avoiding risky business to minimize losses or ending up catching a court case. It marks life coming to an end regarding a terminal illness or having a short life due to lifestyle choices. The person needs to work diligently with the divinities and ancestors to avoid anger issues, heart disease, or other sudden incidentals due to living a stressful life. This is an oracle of avoiding being crooked or influenced by criminal elements or intentions. Iroso is an oracle of traps being laid, hidden agendas, extortion, or blackmail. "If you can't do the time, then don't do the crime." If you like an adrenaline rush and

exposing yourself and others to danger, then be ready to pay for the consequences of those actions. Beware of someone desiring to get rid of you from somewhere, removing, or getting you out of the way for them to take over. Oracle of being let go, fired or no longer desired.

HEXAGRAM

57

57 The Wind, Subtle Penetration

This oracle is a reflection on the movement of the wind. Wind or air penetrates everywhere, and it is necessary for life. It teaches us that a mountain no matter how immovable and strong, a steady breeze with patience and years of constant thrashing will produce a hole, crater, or ditch in it. This is an example of how something bit by bit consistently and constantly in time will produce erosion or were something out. The wind or air must have somewhere to go and changes course when it needs too. But, its direction, strength, or weakening in movement depends on its mission. This means that there must be a purpose, reason, and value to his worth. The wind carries electromagnetic waves, convection, moistures, and all types of particulars at molecular levels. Because of this force there is air travel, communication, information, and commerce. Hence, your penetrating movement cannot be disorganized, spontaneous, and without thought. Because it will be waisted energy that eventually will have to be withdrawn or recovered.

38

38 Opposition

When opposition arrives, one needs to be diligent and advance slowly, not rush, nor push forward spontaneously. This is a time where someone, or something does not blend, mix, unite, and goes against others. Know that when people oppose one another problems will arise. Hence, meeting each other halfway in small matters can lead to better things or problem solving. Look at the benefits of resolving a little bit at a time and make changes that can bring about a positive outcome, even when there is opposition. Finger pointing, arguments, and stubbornness won't solve anything. Coming to terms due to mutual respect and using diplomacy will set things back on track and all will benefit.

0
1
1
0

I Ching tetragram 10 - Agreements; Yoruba Cowrie 15 - Marunla; Yoruba IFa Iwori

Iwori is the oracle of your head's view on things or your head getting around to the right thought processes. It is to know what it means to think; think goodness as much as to know what it is to think evil and be evil. Oracle of never thinking one is a know it all, or to believe they know more than God, his divinities, and the land of the dead. It's the oracle of scientific discovery, technology, psychology, and all-around wisdom. Yet, maintaining a level head being constructive and not destructive. Beware of a mental breakdown due to overexerting one's brain in trying too hard to accomplish desires. It is wisdom to know that what is meant for you comes with little effort. Because it is meant to be and easy, it is right and the right timing too. What is not meant is known because of the struggle that it takes in trying to obtain it, only to lose it because it was not meant to be. The individual must beware of becoming overbearing, autocratic, or tyrannical because one will end up alone. Where privileged individuals can lose everything being overconfident, and making willful mistakes, they need to listen to others too and respect their advice or opinion. The greatest challenge is to learn how to obtain things by the grace of God, and divinities, not thinking all things come just because of your efforts. This demands great patience and allowing the divinities to bring things to you. Iwori's inner or external battle relates to finding their right place in the world. Frustration can come from the inability to uphold a position in society that is recognizable. They have a great need to feel that they are not just contributing to family, community, or society but also leaving a mark. Iwori is an oracle where families destroy one another through infighting, competing, and showing who's the dominate one. Yet, they as a unit become a force to be reckoned with when united or focused on the greater good of the whole family. Individuals should work on forging a legacy that lasts generations in this way they will truly make their mark on life.

HEXAGRAM

58

58 The Joyous Lake

As the name implies joyousness or happiness. It is a time for openness of expression with those of like mind. This oracle represents demonstrating to those that one trust happiness, or that one has reason to be. It is a time for sharing ideas and becoming excited about prospects. But, like all demonstrations or expression, there is a correct way and an incorrect way. The cheerfulness must be sincere, truthful, and never overdone. It must be due to having success in resolving situations and looking forward to contributing to things becoming better. It's not just a celebration for amusement, or seeking pleasure, boasting, or gloating. It is joyousness without conflict, nothing that can lead to jealousy, envy, or distress. Hence, why happiness should be experienced with those that one trust.

37 Family or Group

Blood is thicker than water, and everyone in a family carry mutual traits. Hence, in a family folks must strive towards getting along. Getting along with your family is like getting along with oneself. This is attributed to all members recognizing each other's roles and position; know yourself and what you can contribute to the whole. This begins with a good leader that can motivate and inspire others as well as keep the family organized and intact. All members must maintain good character in meeting individual goals. The family or group is a collective. This means that all have separate responsibilities, but when putting them all together working in common interest, they accomplish optimum goals. Recognition must be given especially to those that have or share in the task of keeping everyone together. In relation to an actual family, one should ask if one believes in family, and if you do, will it require a marriage. Always remember that when forging a family, it becomes something greater than oneself. A family is a legacy, so nothing should be thought of in short term. Legacies are meant to exist long past our existence and withstand the test of generations.

1
0
1
1

I Ching tetragram 05 - Grace; Yoruba Cowrie 16 - Meridilogun; Yoruba IFa Otura

Otura speaks of living in an inhospitable place. It's to be surrounded or live among con artists, and thieves. Also, to avoid being conned or tricked, someone is to be outwitted. Never be the first to know or know the most and the last to take advantage of opportunities. This is a sign of not being given recognition for your efforts or taken for granted. Don't take things for granted, life, family, relationship, jobs, or career, etc. Oracle of being too slow to take advantage of an opportunity due to being distracted. The person needs to have a sharp mind and keep things in order. Not saying you are going to do but doing it, especially with honor. The sooner an individual acquires the necessary skills, and identifies their talents or career, the sooner they will be successful. Oracle prescribes not allowing situations to drag. Bringing closure to situations will allow for one to go on to the next thing without skipping a beat. This sign doesn't permit delaying because carelessness and making mistakes will take hold. Oracle of knowing how to live within your means, respect, and worships the forces of God. How well and proficient individual

works with the divine forces, so will their grace bring them blessings. Speaks of dark forces robbing the person's luck, happiness, and economic well-being when not appeased or expunged in time. Yet, Otura is an oracle of resolving with good luck when situations are taken care of in time. Identify grace, gift, or being gracious in doing things with good taste, will win the hearts of others. And, with this comes the necessary support, not being alone, or left alone with all the weight upon your shoulders.

HEXAGRAM

59

59 Dissolution Dispersion Dissipation Dissolve

Like all motions that come and go. This oracle teaches us to let things go, and for the right reasons. A dissolution is to allow something to dismiss because it is time, even when there has been a letdown. A dispersion has to do with something/someone taking its course, path, or going in a particular direction. There are moments that we are not in agreement, but we must leave it alone. It also implies going on or being a part of a mission. Then, there is a dissipating or subtle release, because it is better to release a little at a time, than something abruptly. Just because there is a dismissal, dissolution, or dispersion does not mean it has to be forever. When a dispersion is with good intentions and part of a well-executed plan. All things can be regathered or return for evaluation, and acknowledgment of its success or failure of mission. Leaving for the sake of change, and gaining new ground, and experiences is also good. Because without experiencing one cannot realize other things. Also, without someone leaving there wouldn't be an opening for someone or something to new to come.

27

27 The Corners of the Mouth

There are good reasons for opening one's mouth, and other reasons for keeping it shut.
This oracle says that we can tell a lot about individuals by what they nourish themselves with. There are those that nourish the belly, those that nourish the mind, those that nourish their bodies, those that nourish spirituality, and those only desire to nourish tongues with gossip and falsehoods. In essence, too much of anything is not good, as in we need a balance even when it comes to what we decide to nourish ourselves with. Food can enter the mouth tasting very good, yet leave the body smelling foul, as in it decays within the digestive system. When is something good for you and when is something just not right or no longer of good taste? We must look around and seek the truths, speak truths, and discern lies. When do certain people or situations cease to provide something that is of worth, useful, and tangible. Actions can cease to be of worth when they don't provide something of value, as in when they hurt others. This is an oracle of working on physical, emotional, psychological, and spiritual well-being, not stigmatization, discrimination, stereotyping, or giving in to hate and prejudices.

0
0
1
0

I Ching tetragram 14 - Purity; Yoruba Cowrie 12 - Eyila; Yoruba IFa Otrupon

Otrupon is to be offended, to offend, or someone is on the offensive. Implying the need to protect yourself. This is an oracle of overcoming traumas; bullied, violated, disrespected, embarrassed, harassed, assaulted, cursed out, or abused. Speaks of wanting out of a relation, situation, job, and unable to find the way out. There is someone that wants to take over or win everything at all costs. They would do whatever it takes to get someone out of their way and obtain their means. Not to give in to selfishness, ego, or pride; also, to never be prejudice, misjudge, nor persecute anyone unjustly. Speaks of family betraying one another. Where mates in a separation battle over possessions and custody to the brinks of destroying one another. After a storm comes to calm as in - we need to weather storms; know how to outlive ordeals. Otrupon is an oracle of peace and harmony returning after having undergone situations of great turmoil and tribulation. With Otrupon one must be very intelligent not to lose while trying to be slicker than the rest. Hence, not to be overconfident in thinking you are getting over on others. As the

same, beware of someone desiring to get over on you in some fashion and gain leverage or advantage over a situation. In this oracle, folks easily forgot the sacrifices that you make for those you love. Hence, folks forget the sacrifices one makes for others in general. Don't be the same lead by example be the better person, but always cover your butt.

HEXAGRAM

60

60 Limitations

We are to recognize limitations and set boundaries. This is not just positive because it is logical, and correct behavior, but for everyone's protection. Limitations imposed that oppress, inhibits freedom, defies logical reasoning is negative. All things negative will sooner or later meet with resistance and conflict. There is a correct way of placing limitations and this is through communicating the reason for the boundaries, and then the effect that it needs to give. When everyone's aware of what behavior is expected everyone can live in harmony and success can be assured.

27

27 The Corners of the Mouth

There are good reasons for opening one's mouth, and other reasons for keeping it shut.
This oracle says that we can tell a lot about individuals by what they nourish themselves with. There are those that nourish the belly, those that nourish the mind, those that nourish their bodies, those that nourish spirituality, and those only desire to nourish tongues with gossip and falsehoods. In essence, too much of anything is not good, as in we need a balance even when it comes to what we decide to nourish ourselves with. Food can enter the mouth tasting very good, yet leave the body smelling foul, as in it decays within the digestive system. When is something good for you and when is something just not right or no longer of good taste? We must look around and seek the truths, speak truths, and discern lies. When do certain people or situations cease to provide something that is of worth, useful, and tangible. Actions can cease to be of worth when they don't provide something of value, as in when they hurt others. This is an oracle of working on physical, emotional, psychological, and spiritual well-being, not stigmatization, discrimination, stereotyping, or giving in to hate and prejudices.

0
0
1
1

I Ching tetragram 13 - Success; Yoruba Cowrie 11 - Ojuani; Yoruba IFa Ojuani

Ojuani means from riches to rags, and from rags to riches. It's an oracle of doubts, complexes, and potential insecurities. Persons have an overzealous ambition that when not held back can become destructive. Oracle where person's must keep their ego in check. Learn to live with others in peace strive for an education obtaining a career profession, or title. To be a responsible and not a careless individual, beware of desires; we can't have everything or everything we think is good for us might not be. Oracle of becoming easily bored with mates, so beware of promiscuity and STDs. People lose due to jealousy, and envy within a circle of friendships, work, and even family. Speaks of dark forces getting in the way of progress, external or internal. Oracle marks needing to be exorcised of dark energies/forces when prevalent i.e., noticed through not sleeping well, feeling haunted, or energy being sucked out of you. Beware of people that cling to you and become like a parasite, just as you should not be a parasite to anyone. Being sucked dry is noticed by how much you're losing due to relationship/business; not just money

but also one's peace of mind, tranquility, or space. In this oracle, one's family or mate's family can be your worst enemy or the biggest asset depending on how much they care about you or love you. Oracle of hurting or injuring the one we love through our actions or not noticing that one is doing this. Beware of being head-strung and willful as in my way or the highway. One must be flexible or understand when one has encountered inflexible individuals that don't contribute to positive things but get in the way and disrupt one's happiness. Beware of justice situations through being involved with people that are into illegal activities. Beware of becoming involved in illegal activities due to not acquiring a career in time. Oracle of never being envious of others, oracle of knowing who's on your side, and not damaging relationships.

HEXAGRAM

61

61 Inner Truth

Being honest with oneself leads to being honest with others. The practice of inner truth is beyond just telling or accepting the truth. It is one of self-analysis, self-criticism, and the will to change when knowing one is incorrect. We live in a world where people believe lies and are expected to accept it. This begins with lying to oneself and accepting denial. There is no greater proof of ignorance than this kind of attitude, character, or behavior. Persons such as this can never be trusted, and the best thing one can do is leave their side. Because, one day arguments, quarrels, and foolishness will follow. This can become very dangerous and can be avoided just through recognizing those that can't admit the truth to themselves or others.

27 The Corners of the Mouth

There are good reasons for opening one's mouth, and other reasons for keeping it shut.

This oracle says that we can tell a lot about individuals by what they nourish themselves with. There are those that nourish the belly, those that nourish the mind, those that nourish their bodies, those that nourish spirituality, and those only desire to nourish tongues with gossip and falsehoods. In essence, too much of anything is not good, as in we need a balance even when it comes to what we decide to nourish ourselves with. Food can enter the mouth tasting very good, yet leave the body smelling foul, as in it decays within the digestive system. When is something good for you and when is something just not right or no longer of good taste? We must look around and seek the truths, speak truths, and discern lies. When do certain people or situations cease to provide something that is of worth, useful, and tangible. Actions can cease to be of worth when they don't provide something of value, as in when they hurt others. This is an oracle of working on physical, emotional, psychological, and spiritual well-being, not stigmatization, discrimination, stereotyping, or giving in to hate and prejudices.

0
0
1
1

I Ching tetragram 13 - Success; Yoruba Cowrie 11 - Ojuani; Yoruba IFa Ojuani

Ojuani means from riches to rags, and from rags to riches. It's an oracle of doubts, complexes, and potential insecurities. Persons have an overzealous ambition that when not held back can become destructive. Oracle where person's must keep their ego in check. Learn to live with others in peace strive for an education obtaining a career profession, or title. To be a responsible and not a careless individual, beware of desires; we can't have everything or everything we think is good for us might not be. Oracle of becoming easily bored with mates, so beware of promiscuity and STDs. People lose due to jealousy, and envy within a circle of friendships, work, and even family. Speaks of dark forces getting in the way of progress, external or internal. Oracle marks needing to be exorcised of dark energies/forces when prevalent i.e., noticed through not sleeping well, feeling haunted, or energy being sucked out of you. Beware of people that cling to you and become like a parasite, just as you should not be a parasite to anyone. Being sucked dry is noticed by how much you're losing due to relationship/business; not just money

but also one's peace of mind, tranquility, or space. In this oracle, one's family or mate's family can be your worst enemy or the biggest asset depending on how much they care about you or love you. Oracle of hurting or injuring the one we love through our actions or not noticing that one is doing this. Beware of being head-strung and willful as in my way or the highway. One must be flexible or understand when one has encountered inflexible individuals that don't contribute to positive things but get in the way and disrupt one's happiness. Beware of justice situations through being involved with people that are into illegal activities. Beware of becoming involved in illegal activities due to not acquiring a career in time. Oracle of never being envious of others, oracle of knowing who's on your side, and not damaging relationships.

HEXAGRAM

62

62 Preponderance of the Small, Succeeding through Small Favors

It is better to do or achieve lots of little bits at a time, then one big thing some of the time. With consistency in small matters, one will achieve great things. This oracle implies not taking risks, but to concentrate on what is sure rather than doubtful. It is not a time of taking a leap of faith. This is how we know that something is doubtful when we are unsure. This oracle signifies to play it safe, to take a modest approach to situations and avoid trouble. Do not allow anyone to distract you from the consistency in gains that you can achieve doing things slower. Especially, if you know that all things are working, slowly but surely. Avoid provocations, intimidations, and temptations, this will lead to setbacks.

28

28 - Preponderance of the Great - Excessiveness or Extra

Oracle of excessiveness, extra, too much to handle, or overindulging. This also means too beware of gluttony, greed, or exaggeration. The advice is to understand when something is too much, overkill, or know when something is being overdone. Something will break when it is in excess, it stresses that all things must be handled correctly and with care for what things to not break. Proper due diligence (homework), evaluations, and executions will give way to successful outcome. Excess, or extra is good when it meets expectations or surpasses them. Preponderance of the great also means to accept change or know that change is unavoidable no matter how much we try to push forward or hold back. The individual might want to but forces more powerful are pushing for things to manifest despite of attempting to control them.

1
1
0
0

I Ching tetragram 03 - Enthusiasm; Yoruba Cowrie 04 - Iroso;
Yoruba IFa Iroso

Iroso means the unknown, mysterious, hidden, secrets, and surprises. This is a sign of riches, obtaining, inheriting, or achieving status. It's to avoid entrapments of being made part of a grander scheme. Iroso has a saying, "No one knows the mysteries that lie beneath the depths of the seas." As in a blessing, which can come out of nowhere; as well as trouble when taken in a negative context. It's an oracle of discovery as much as it is of exposure to danger. It announces a business takeover or being taken advantage of. It recommends avoiding risky business to minimize losses or ending up catching a court case. It marks life coming to an end regarding a terminal illness or having a short life due to lifestyle choices. The person needs to work diligently with the divinities and ancestors to avoid anger issues, heart disease, or other sudden incidentals due to living a stressful life. This is an oracle of avoiding being crooked or influenced by criminal elements or intentions. Iroso is an oracle of traps being laid, hidden agendas, extortion, or blackmail. "If you can't do the time, then don't do the crime." If you like an adrenaline rush and

exposing yourself and others to danger, then be ready to pay for the consequences of those actions. Beware of someone desiring to get rid of you from somewhere, removing, or getting you out of the way for them to take over. Oracle of being let go, fired or no longer desired.

HEXAGRAM

63

63 After Completion, Completed

This oracle signifies taking a break after completing tasks, ventures, assignments, or milestone achievement. This is a time to get reorganized for the next plan or strategy that needs execution. The break is for a visualization of the future an outreach mental assessment of what is to follow. Physical labor does not need to be included at this time just the brainstorming that leads to proper organization of ideas. It is also forward thinking for clarity in direction in way things should go and staying ahead. The oracle advises to completely resolve all outstanding issues, so that any new venture can begin on a clean slate. Never carry old baggage to new situations, you will be contaminating it, in essence extending what should have been complete. This defeats the purpose of starting something new.

64

64 Before Completion

One can never be overzealous in starting a new venture, when one has not fully completed the previous one. This is an oracle of cross checking and marking things along the way as they complete. Ask yourself what is missing to complete? Then, take things from there. Things cannot be accomplished before its time, or until all work or job is done. This is true in all phases of transition, change, or new things to come. There is a proper way of bringing closure and that is not being careless. Admit when somethings are not ready, and incomplete to bring closure. Holding back or showing restraint is not a bad thing. It's better to be sure than doubtful, or better to be safe than sorry. Also, just because you can sense or feel the completion and it's within grasp, doesn't mean to relax. Cross checking requires being meticulous.

0
1
0
1

I Ching tetragram 11 - Limitations; Yoruba Cowrie 10 - Ofun;
Yoruba IFa Ofun

Ofun is an oracle of self-defense, where defending yourself
is permitted. It's an oracle of great wisdom, growth, and
grandeur. Yet, not to allow the grandeur to get one's head, or it
will cause failures and setbacks. This oracle stresses seeking
perfection and balance. In essence, greatness without humility or
not knowing limitations will lead to demise and destruction. This
oracle personifies living in harmony with society, nature, and your
surroundings - Tao. It's where God's messengers/holy
scriptures/words and testaments enter the world to teach
mankind how to better live. Signifies losing one's life accidentally,
or by mistake. Oracle recommends never overstepping one's
position, being disobedient, taking unnecessary risk, or imposing
will on others. This is an oracle of understanding boundaries,
limitations, and knowing which lines are never too cross. What
comes to mind with this oracle is "You're only as strong as the
next person, which is equal to you or stronger." Ofun is an oracle
of recognizing we can't know everything; we can't have
everything, and we will lose thinking we are everything. Beware of

stepping out of line with one's actions or misjudging individuals. Oracle of being mindful of one's actions and the consequences that they can cause, as well as the actions of others along the same lines. With this oracle we learn to understand the nature of death. As in the cycle of a disease individual that slowly deteriorates leading to death. This cycle includes the individual and family coping with the process, beginning with denial, anger, anxiety, depression, acceptance, and finally grief. The spiritual process begins with death (reapers) coming to meet, hopefully in a controlled way, but as we know death can be sudden too. Then, the crossing over, extends to family acknowledging their ancestors, and initiating spiritual practices for the transcendence of their souls. Ofun represents processes involving the land of the dead, working with the dead, elevation or crossing over of the dead through ancestor worship.

HEXAGRAM

64

64 Before Completion

One can never be overzealous in starting a new venture, when one has not fully completed the previous one. This is an oracle of cross checking and marking things along the way as they complete. Ask yourself what is missing to complete? Then, take things from there. Things cannot be accomplished before its time, or until all work or job is done. This is true in all phases of transition, change, or new things to come. There is a proper way of bringing closure and that is not being careless. Admit when somethings are not ready, and incomplete to bring closure. Holding back or showing restraint is not a bad thing. It's better to be sure than doubtful, or better to be safe than sorry. Also, just because you can sense or feel the completion and it's within grasp, doesn't mean to relax. Cross checking requires being meticulous.

63

63 After Completion, Completed

This oracle signifies taking a break after completing tasks, ventures, assignments, or milestone achievement. This is a time to get reorganized for the next plan or strategy that needs execution. The break is for a visualization of the future an outreach mental assessment of what is to follow. Physical labor does not need to be included at this time just the brainstorming that leads to proper organization of ideas. It is also forward thinking for clarity in direction in way things should go and staying ahead. The oracle advises to completely resolve all outstanding issues, so that any new venture can begin on a clean slate. Never carry old baggage to new situations, you will be contaminating it, in essence extending what should have been complete. This defeats the purpose of starting something new.

1
0
1
0

I Ching tetragram 06 - Dissolution; Yoruba Cowrie 05 - Oche;
Yoruba IFa Oche

Oracle of the blood being thicker than water, blood being the transporter of cells for living organisms to function. In essence, blood is life. Oracle where money came into the world, and today is the lifeblood of society, business, commerce, or government economies. This is an oracle of fights over money, and in some cases over livelihood (bringing food to your table). Oracle of being cheated or feeling cheated. It's the oracle where the money is cursed, or "the root to all evil." Human blood feeds money i.e., the blood sweat, and tears of those that work to survive. Rich folks curse it because many of them don't want to lose it. Poor folks curse it because they don't have it, and it eludes them. In Oche negativity stems from the decomposition of things, corruption, failures, when situations fall apart. Uncleanliness, impurities, or filthiness corrupts and generates diseases. Hence, sanitize, wash, purify, and never allow germs, parasites, or viruses to take hold. Taking care of one's digestion, and blood is important to avoid illnesses or diseases from an early age. Oche is an oracle of dysfunctional, disorganized family, relationships, or

affairs. The protection of the family, economic position, and not allowing for relationship problems getting in the way of happiness is key to being successful. In this oracle one is to make one's spirituality stronger through dedication, devotion, and being responsible with one's gift; otherwise, one loses the gift and gives way to the decomposition of all things. Oche is an oracle of protecting that which you've worked so hard to maintain. Love God and his divinities so you attend them, so will they support you in getting out of situations and resolving for better living. Oche is an oracle of needing to be saved through taking a leap of faith and entering a shamanistic priestly way of life.

Appendix

The Bigrams – the four elements and their attributes:

FIRE	AIR	WATER	EARTH
Summer	Spring	Winter	Fall
77 or 99	69, 67,89, 87	96,98,76,78	66, 88
Old Yang	Young Yang	Young Yin	Old Yin
Yes – Affirmative	Yes – Work Needed	No – Work Needed	No - Affirmative
Speaking Here: Soul, Spirituality, Consciousness, Religion, Politics, Your destiny, path, or journey - Head	Speaks Here: Mind, intellect, wisdom, psychology, Science, medicine, Communication - Mouth	Speaks Here: Feelings, emotions, justice, injustice, socializing, relationships – Heart and Eyes	Speaks Here: Physical Form, health, materialism, economics, ancestors, rituals – Feet and body

The Trigrams – observable phenomena and their attributes:

Ch'ien – Sky – Father – Creative – Heaven		01 – Position South, Element Metal – Old Yang Spirit, head, soul, seeds, strengths, religion, politics, above, external divine power, God universal life force; Father
Tui – Dui – Joyous Lake/Marsh		02 – Position Southeast, Element Metal: Young Yin Happiness, well-being, good health, positive emotions, optimism, reflections, openness, internal. Youngest daughter
Li – Clinging Fire – Sun		03 – Position East, Element Fire – Young Yang Obtaining, grabbing, holding, hunting, protecting, above, external, seeking, necessary and careful, light giving, middle daughter

Chen – Zen – Thunder – Arousing		04 – Position Northeast, Element Wood – Old Yin Movement, Striking, Shocking, things manifest, fast, movement, paths; Eldest Son
Sun – Xun – The Gentle - Wind		05 – Position Southwest, Element Wood – Old Yang Penetrating, communication, information, travel, invisible, unseen, creativity, above, external; Eldest daughter
K'an – Kan – Abysmal – Water - Moon		06 – Position West, Element Water – Old Yang Darkness, negativity, dangers, emotional, external, hidden, illness, difficult to control; Middle son
Ken – Gen – Mountain – Keeping Still		07 – Position Northwest, Element Earth – Young Yang Resting, stationary, elevation, growth, immovable, stand still, landmark,

		extension, external; Youngest Son
K'un – Kun – Earth – Receptive – Devoted		08 – Position North, Element Earth – Old Yin Crops, Harvest, yielding, giving, burial, land of the dead, ancestors, matter, materialization, commerce, receiving, below, tolerance, life & death, the body; Mother

Metal	Ch'ien and Tui – melts, molds, shape shifts, flexible when heated, hard when cold, goes from rigid to manageable
Earth	K'un and Ken – Ageless, everlasting, ever giving, maturity, acceptance, nurturing, loyal. Security, bonding, wisdom, strength, People, materialism, the masses
Fire	Li – Separates, chemical breakdown, heat, pleasures, desires, seeking, vigor, holding, capturing, gives light, ignites, combustion, energy, generate or destroy
Water	Harsh, difficult, unforeseen, hidden, roots, sprouting, seeds, plants, insect, germination, growth, immaturity, introvert, realization
Wood	Chen and Sun – Cutting through, pushing, flowing,

	gives or uses energy, extrovert, vision, visualize, support, help, build, feeding, necessary

The Tetragrams

The attributes of the Tetragrams are derived from their respect Bigram and Trigram symbols. The two Bigrams at the top of the four-line tetragram are the four elements. The two bottom lines of the bigrams are the four elements copulating with one another. You can attribute the trigrams to each tetragram by noticing the bottom three lines of the tetragram.

Old Yang, Heaven, Summer, South, and Fire:

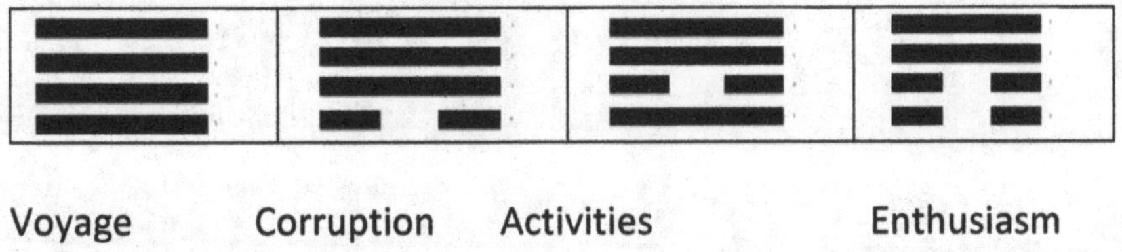

Voyage   Corruption   Activities   Enthusiasm

Young Yang, Spring, East, and Air
11

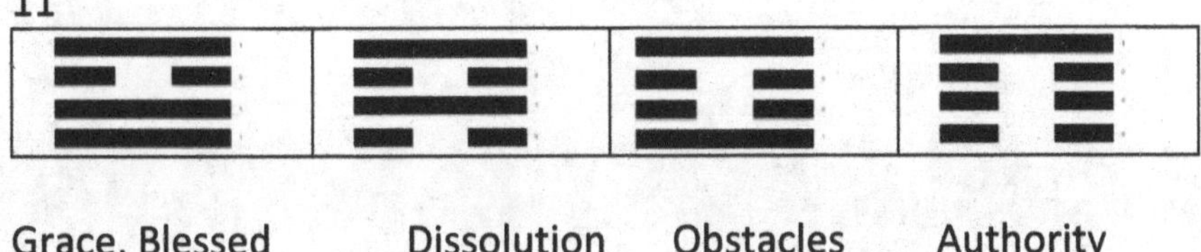

Grace, Blessed   Dissolution   Obstacles   Authority

Young Yin, Winter, West, and Water

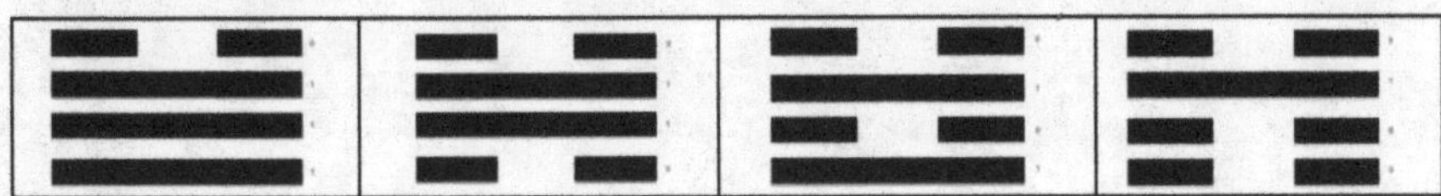

Old Yin, Earth, Fall, North, and Earth

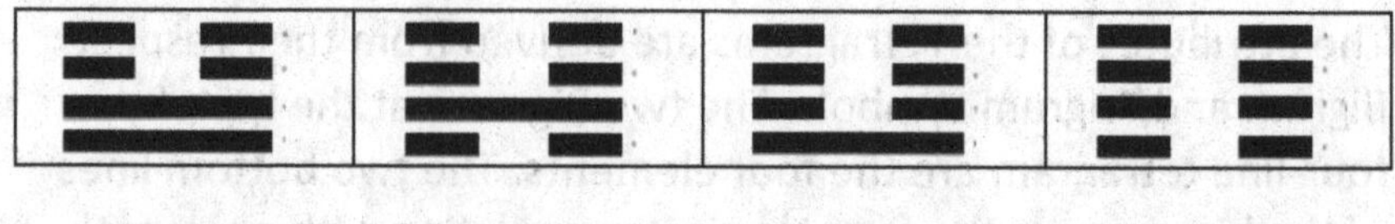

| Success | Purity | Failure | Materialism |

References

Novaton, S (1984). Sixto J. Novaton initial studies and observations into the I Ching logic

Walker, B. B. (1992). The I Ching or Book of Changes. New York, NY: St. Martin's Press

Wilhelm, R., Baynes, C.F., (1978). The I Ching Book of Changes. Princeton, NJ: Princeton University Press

www.ingramcontent.com/pod-product-compliance
Lightning Source LLC
LaVergne TN
LVHW031428170726
843492LV00010B/2901